Remnants

A Post-Apocalyptic Epic in Verse by E. C. Mira

Copyright © 2025 E. C. Mira

All rights reserved. No part of this publication may be reproduced, distributed, or transmitted in any form by any means without the written permission of the publisher except for the use of brief quotations in a book review.

For my son

who never wants to go to bed on time,

and in doing so,

gave me the quiet nights to write this.

Table of Contents

Preface 6

The Before 24

    Canto I 25

The First Howl 40

    Canto II 56

The Break 86

    Canto III 117

Origins Unnamed 128

Against the Quiet 148

    Canto IV 158

Sanctioned Breaths 176

    Canto V 178

Betrayal & Fire 194

    Canto VI 201

The Ones who Chose Not To 228

The Hollowing 248

    Canto VII 250

Archives of the Unspoken 280

Liturgies of the Unrested 314

Last Breath, First Word 350

    Canto VIII 357

O Muse, O Echo

Echo, not of gods,
but of what could not stay.
Return to me in fragments.
Return in breath,
in footprint,
in doors left half-ajar.

I do not seek the first sound
only its trail.
The voice that bounced off ruin
and decided not to come back whole.

Be my muse not in music,
but in warning,
in repetition,
in what tries again because it cannot rest.

I will not name you.
But I will listen.
And I will write down what you say
when no one else remains to hear it.

I did not begin this book to chronicle horror.
Not solely.
Horror is a shadow, yes.
But it is shaped by the light behind it:
memory, hunger, love, and loss.

This world is not gone, it is becoming.
Becoming soil, becoming silence, becoming myth.
Where the living struggle to remember their names,
and the dead learn new ways to speak.

What follows is not a record of victories.
It is not tidy. It is not fair.
These are the remains
of what survives after even fire.
Each poem is a breath I didn't think I'd take.
Each line a step when there was nowhere safe to go.

And if you're reading this now,
you've survived enough to listen.
Let us begin.
Not with the first scream
but with the last breath, still trembling in defiance.

The Last Poet

Preface

I do not write for memory,
but fire.
The tongue forgets
what silence teaches first.
Beneath this dust,
there once were words like blood
warm,
fast,
and loud with names
we dare not speak.

Silence After Fire

They came like storms that rotted out the sun.
The cities fell like teeth from brittle gums.
The dead rose slow, and then the fight begun.

No scream could hold what history becomes.
The towers slouched and shed their glass like skin.
A fire fed on law and church and drums.

The earth grew soft beneath the growing din.
We buried light beneath collapsing stone.
We sang of peace with blood beneath the chin.

And I, the last, the poet left alone,
emerged from sleep beneath a tilted train
with journal pages soaked to pulp and bone.

The ash hung thick, as constant as the rain.
The moon was dull, as if ashamed to glow.
The clocks were bent. The sirens sang in vain.

I wandered through a house where none could go
its frames were warped; porcelain dolls left in the dark.
One photo stood, unbroken in the snow.

It showed a child with eyes too wide, too stark,
and parents framed by leaves and Sunday suits.
A world erased but paused within that spark.

I found old fruit still hanging on its roots.
It crumbled when I touched it, turned to smoke.
The cars were vines. The stores were tombs of boots.

One playground held a slide like spines that broke.
A swing moved gently, slow without a cause.
A voice replayed a birthday song it spoke.

Each word was caught, unfinished by the pause
of death mid-breath. The candles still were wax.
A knife lay near, untouched by hands or laws.

The silence came with pressure, not with lacks.
It pressed the ribs, it echoed in the knees.
It held the bones like well-behaved attacks.

I walked for hours past the stripped marquees.
The posters told of shows that never played.
The actors smiled, untouched by this disease.

One station blared, its screens still in cascade
of news from days before the sky turned red:
"No cause yet found for sickness's new shade."

They did not know how fast the sickness spread.
It whispered. It persuaded cells to sleep.
It turned the soul to something darkly fed.

It did not shout. It did not charge or leap.
It moved like thought unnoticed, like a doubt.
It loved the places quiet, cold, and deep.

One man I knew had tried to warn the route
he wrote in chalk on sidewalks, "boil the air."
His body bloomed with black around his mouth.

One nurse I watched broke glass to make a stair.
She climbed until the roof fell under flame.
She vanished like a breath too thin to spare.

A child once pointed, but forgot the name
of what she saw a tree, a bird, a sun.
The words collapsed. They dropped out of the frame.

And me? I walked with verses not yet done.
I scrawled in soot across a chapel door:
"They burned the sky and left us what they shun."

I met a boy who knew not what came before.
He called the stars "the holes where night leaks out."
He kissed a corpse, then walked into the floor.

Some wept. Some sang. Some simply turned about.
Some counted breaths the way we once used clocks.
Some built their homes in caves beneath the drought.

One girl wore masks made out of broken socks.
She named each one. She taught them all to pray.
She left where the blood ran through the rocks.

A merchant shouted, "One more deal, one day!"
He sold illusions drawn on bits of glass.
He said, "Forget the end it's just decay."

And I, who stayed, who did not let it pass,
have carved these stanzas into ash and air.
They may not hold, but still they mark, they last.

*They say a silence deep enough can speak
not loud, but like a floorboard's ghostly creak.*

*I've wandered through the ribs of cities torn,
and found in ash the echo of the worn.*

*Their names are gone, but still I feel the bend
where someone wept and touched the world's last end.*

*I did not start with purpose, only need
to write the death of gods that made us bleed.*

*No cure is scrawled in what I leave behind.
No wisdom, just the record of the blind.*

*But still I write, because I saw them fall
the kind, the cruel, the child curled in a stall.*

*Each one, a line. Each loss, a broken rhyme.
I write. Because forgetting is a crime.*

*The world has rotted through its final verse,
but poems breathe beneath the patient curse.*

*They walk with me, these syllables of dead
they whisper in the marrow of my tread.*

I've etched their faces onto bark and bone.
I write not hope, but proof they died unknown.

Perhaps the proof is hope in its disguise.
A name half-whispered never fully dies.

No hero am I. No prophet, saint, or sage.
I only burn the truths I see onto the page.

And if these stanzas vanish in the dust,
then let them die as all the dying must

but not before they carry one small spark,
across the void, beneath the godless dark.

Skyfall

I saw the sky once tear along its seams,
not with a scream, but hunger wrapped in skin.
And we, with lungs of salt and bone-stitched fear,
we sang. We sang until the light turned black.

We buried the world.
We buried the noise.
Still, it walked

A woman screamed inside her wedding dress.
The veil stuck to her face. The fire blessed.

I am the last to name the ones who burned.
The cities sleep but dreaming makes them howl.
The pages curl with every breath I take.
My ink is ash. My script, the bones of gods.

The stars, no longer stars,
watched as we cut our shadows from our feet
sewed them to the dead so they stay
inside the dirt we prayed was still a tomb.

But the earth is soft. and the night is long.

And nothing rots as fast as faith when fed.
Don't scream. Don't breathe. Don't stop.
(that was our song once)

I do not tell you how the plague began.
I am no healer, priest, or truth's dry hand.
I only know what rose when light withdrew
and walked.
And fed.
And learned the taste of prayers.

O children born in silence, let me speak.
O fire that swallows syllables like flesh,
let me remember ruin into rhyme.

For songs may break, but silence breaks us more.
This is the book of ash.
This is the verse of what would not stay dead.
This is the elegy the fire could not eat.

Come closer now.
I have a story
and it has teeth.

They burned their gods and wore the smoke as thread.
Then prayed to sticks, to teeth, to dolls instead.

Their words grew warped, their tongues forgot the shape
of "once" and "why" they only learned escape.

They spoke in fragments, grunts, and gestures torn.
Their grammar died. But still, a sound was born.

Not truth, not grace, but something in between
a language scraped from hunger, ash, and spleen.

And me, I watched and wrote it as I could.
Not holy, no. But still I called it good.

For even shattered voices seek release
and even gods in ruins ask for peace.

Intercession

Forgive the ruined
grammar of the dead.
Our mouths were never
made for this decay.

In alleyways,
we built new alphabets
from broken jawbones
and a child's hum.

One syllable was "stay."
One syllable was "gone."
The difference
burned inside the throat

And some of us still
whispered to the sky,
though stars were
only teeth behind a veil.

One woman wrapped
her prayers around a stick
and called it "God."

That stick still walks.
We do not ask how.

They say the mind decays
slower than skin.

I watched my brother
name the moon "our house."
I watched him feed
a doll and call it "mom."

I wrote him once a poem.
He ate it.

Bring Fire

You ask why I still write.
You think the ink is mourning.
It is not.
It is a weapon carved from memory.
We live in stories now. Or else, we die.

I name what fed us.
I name what turned back.
I name the breathless kiss that still remembers
the shape of lips.
The song that chewed the throat.
I name the sun that would not rise again.

This is the verse of blackened silk.
The world did not end.
It just stopped telling the truth.
If I speak, you must follow.
If you follow, bring fire.

They asked me once what silence truly meant.
I said: the place where color pays its rent.

Where red is not a warning, but a name.
Where gold recalls the mail before it came.

Black does not end. It folds.
It hums in ribs. It lingers in the mold.

Where green grows back, but crooked from the fire,
and orange still dreams it won't become a pyre.

I do not list these hues for beauty's sake.
Each one's a bruise the world forgot to fake.

I write them down because they do not lie.
They stay when memory begins to die.

You think a color's just a way to see.
But I have bled in tones you can't decree.

So if you walk this story's final hum,
prepare your eyes. The colors always come.

Let the Colors Come

The world did not end in black or flame.
It ended in colors, each one slow,
like a wound that bloomed from the inside out.

First came Gold, still warm in the mouth,
sweet with bread and unopened mail,
a lullaby too soft to carry warning.

Then Red, which spoke without tongue,
a stain, a cough, a hallway light,
something we named too late.

Then Black, not void, but verdict
the sound that forgot how to echo.
And taught the silence how to stay

Then Gray, and we walked through it,
ghosts with bones, carrying hunger like hope,
shoes made of silence.

Then White, clean as a cut,
the kind of order that bleeds without color,
a sanctuary dressed in denial.

Then Orange, which needed
no permission, just fuel, and
a reason to forget what the match knew.

And last comes Green, not healing, but memory's twin,
the thing that grows back different,
strange, still reaching.

Let the doors be named.
Let the verses bleed.
Let the colors come.

The Pen is Mightier

We did not have firepower.
But we had
memory.
And ink that dried
even when blood did not.

They took our cities.
They burned the houses
But what we wrote down
stayed.

Paper remembers
what the world forgets.

We did not fight to win.

We wrote
so no one could
say it didn't happen.

We wrote
because silence
was already trying
to revise us.

The Before

The bread still rose without instruction.
The curtains breathed in morning
like it was owed.
Children dropped their backpacks at the door
and forgot them
in the joy of returning.
We said things like "later" and meant them.
We filled our cups with silence,
the good kind,
the kind that never imagined
being broken.

Canto I – The Hour We Thought We Owned

The sky was soft, the coffee warm, the trains
still groaned along their rusted morning lines.
We watched the day arrive between windowpanes.

A woman yelled, but only at the signs
that flashed the bus was late by seven more.
Her life, she swore, was ruled by bad designs.

The man beside her stared down at the floor,
ignoring news that blinked across his phone
a cough in Prague, a lockdown by the shore.

But no one changed the locks. No seeds were sown.
We thought the world too stubborn to dissolve.
What passed for fear was simply overblown.

A child played tag, unsure who would evolve
into the monster half a joke, half true.
The teacher clapped. The children did not solve

the rules but laughed when one forgot her cue.
A girl in yellow spun beneath the trees.
Her mother smiled, then turned away, as you

might glance when traffic pauses just to tease.
No danger, just delay. A signal caught.
The sky above remained its perfect freeze.

A pigeon fluttered. Sirens did not rot
the silence yet. A man sold hot dogs still.
The fire alarms showed nothing to be sought.

I watched it all. I stood upon the hill
that overlooked the waking city's grin.
I wrote not what I feared but what stood still.

The window dressings. Children's teeth. The tin
of mints left open in the market aisle.
The engine hums. The price of aspirin.

A screen went black, then bright, then stayed awhile.
A shape moved through the crowd too slow to miss.
A woman frowned. A boy returned her smile.

That moment held no scream. No crack. No hiss.
Just breath that paused like clocks about to chime.
Just laughter with a loosened emphasis.

And though I did not mark the death of time,
I wrote its weight as though it might return.
I knew too well the power of a rhyme.

The church bell rang. It never felt like a burn.
The pigeons circled once, then veered away.
The lights still worked. The trash men stayed on turn.

A woman sang above a game café.
Her voice was hoarse, but still it held its key.
A boy threw rocks. The ripples did not stay.

I stood beside a man who said to me:
It's calm like this before a summer storm.
He left. He waved. He vanished through debris

not yet collapsed, not yet in breaking form.
The world, you see, does not collapse in sound.
It bows. It shifts. It simmers before warm

turns into heat, and heat into the ground
beneath our lives, which waits for no repair.
It swells in silence. Then it wraps around.

A dog began to bark at open air.
A jogger paused, then tightened both his shoes.
The breeze turned sharp. The paper boy just stared.

A mother kissed her child and checked the news.
The signal blinked. The anchor cleared her throat.
They cut away before she read the cues.

A city bus passed by a church in coat
of scaffolding the work half-done, half-ruined.
A rat emerged with string inside its throat.

No one believed what hadn't yet been ruined.
We told ourselves that we would understand
once danger came, once chaos was in tune.

But when it came, it did not raise a hand.
It did not howl or cry or wear a name.
It moved like fog. It curled around the land.

And I the one who saw, who did not claim
to save, but stayed to write the air we breathed
I watched the world repeat its quiet game.

I marked the hour still in iron sheathed,
when none of us believed it would ignite.
The last full breath we took was not bequeathed.

We never knew which moment turned to night.
And so I write, because that still feels right.

Our Beloved Life

O beloved traffic, your metallic chorus,
humming beneath
our bedroom window
like a lullaby reversed

I worship the bus brakes,
the hiss of tires
slick with yesterday's rain,
the man on the corner
who sells burned coffee
and calls everyone "chief."

Praise to the toast we burned,
to the voicemail your mother left,
to the unopened bill with your name wrong.

And to you
brushing your teeth
in the mirror
that fogs like a secret

I offer my hallelujahs,
quiet and unrepentant.

We were rich in socks with holes,
in calendars we forgot to cross,
in mugs stained with small routines.

There were wars, yes,
but somewhere else.

And there was love,
not loud,
but everywhere.

We had no word for before,
No need for one
after was still in someone else's throat

They watered plants. They checked the daily news.
They never thought to count how much they'd lose.

The world was loud with joy and late alarms.
I wrote it down, its clutter and its charms.

They called it peace, and maybe they were right.
But peace can hide small fractures in the light.

Morning in Pieces

Toast blackened.
The eggs were right.
The train was late, but still arrived.
A child forgot her spelling test.
A man proposed.
A dove took flight.
The world was bored, not cursed or blessed
just quiet in its perfect wrong.
We didn't know we'd passed the best.

We thought the broken toast was all we'd lose.
We laughed when storms delayed the local news.

A child forgot her test, and still she played.
The world was wrong, but wrong in human shade.

I would give anything to fail like that
to burn the eggs and leave the fridge half-flat.

The peace we had was never brave or true,
but soft enough to wrap around the blue.

No flags, no threats, just coffee on the sill
a love that didn't save, but knew how to fill.

And now, when silence thickens into grace,
I write that morning back into this place.

Before We Named It Peace

The kettle hummed beside a cooling cup,
and nothing urgent moved beyond our street.
You smiled without remembering my name;
I loved you more for needing only breath.
We touched like habits hiding in our hands,
then curled beneath the weightless cloth of sleep.

Outside, a siren held its breath in sleep,
the world still measured by the heat of cup.
The wind ran fingers through the garden's hands,
and shoes still filled the quiet of the street.
We woke each morning sure we had the breath
to hold the news and still forget its name.

I wrote a list, forgot to sign my name,
then laughed and fell into another sleep.
You told the dog to sit beneath your breath
and reached for me before you reached your cup.
We'd walk, sometimes, just walking down the street
no destination, just the pulse of hands.

We didn't know the weight inside our hands,
the paper masks, the word that earned no name.
The city hid its future in the street.
The sky was still a friend who watched us sleep.
Our only weapon then was warmth, and cup,
and how we folded light into our breath.

We never thought to question how the breath
might turn, or what could vanish from our hands.
A fever whispered once into a cup
and disappeared before it found a name.
The dusk returned us gently toward our sleep,
the lamplight soft across the painted street.

The mail was late. No danger crossed the street.
We read the stats, then laughed to catch our breath.
We kissed and pressed our luck into our sleep,
still tracing tiny futures on our hands.
We knew the world, though not its final name,
and stirred the sugar gently in the cup.

So let this cup remember nights of deep sleep.
Let hands recall the corners of the street.
Let every breath still carry what we'd name.

It Shattered

A glass left untouched
hums with light
from the window.
No one hears the crack.

The sky keeps its blue
a little too perfectly.
Dogs begin to bark.
With nothing around
to set them off

Someone coughs once.
Twice.
A child forgets her own name.
Birds fly south
They do not return.

A mother hummed and trimmed the dying leaves.
A man rehearsed his lies in crisped-up sleeves.

Two lovers fought in front of building ten
then laughed too loud, then made up again.

The breeze was warm. The mailman wore short sleeves.
A car alarm went off, then ceased to grieve.

An old man cursed the sky for being clear.
A siren rang then passed. It wasn't near.

A chalk hopscotch was scuffed by careless feet.
A girl sat down. Her ice cream met the street.

At noon, the sun arrived without a sound.
No shadows moved. The light just held its ground.

A woman missed her train but didn't care.
A child stood too still in open air.

The streetlamps blinked before they had to light.
A crow took off like something wasn't right.

The breeze came back. The silence wore a grin.
And every door forgot who walked within.

no sirens yet

we woke at seven,
as always.
the coffee pot coughed
like a memory.
outside, light climbed buildings
like it belonged.
someone honked.
someone watered their small plant.
the news said nothing new.
the sky agreed.
toast. teeth. keys in the bowl. kiss at the door.
the trains ran late, but ran.
a dog barked.
a headline folded, unread.
mail fell through.
our shadows stood where they always had.
no sirens yet.
no ash on windowsills.
just time, passing,
like it always meant to.

The Hours Were Full of Light

The hours were full of light and bread,
The radios hummed songs we did not fear.
We kissed like time had nowhere else to tread.

Children chalked suns on every wall they read.
The rain was warm. The rooftops rang out clear.
The hours were full of light and bread.

Each window caught the gold the morning bled.
A letter came, and love was always near.
We kissed like time had nowhere else to tread.

Our gardens bloomed where evening softly led.
The birds returned. The neighbors passed us beer.
The hours were full of light and bread.

No sirens yet, no rumors of the dead
Just birthdays, ovens, schoolyards full of cheer.
We kissed like time had nowhere else to tread.

We lit no candles. Nothing had been said.
The sky wore nothing darker than a tear.
The hours were full of light and bread.
We kissed like time had nowhere else to tread

The First Howl

It began without thunder.
A shiver in the newsprint.
A cough in aisle seven.

We turned up the volume
instead of listening.
Blood is quiet,
until it isn't.

The Restless

They dragged their feet like clocks denied their gears.
Their moans were not of rage, but fractured song.
They moved in flocks, like time composed of fears.

Some wore their wedding bands, still held on wrong.
One had a doll sewn tight into his chest.
They never slept. They never stayed for long.

Their hunger was not simple, not just quest
for meat or blood or brains, as tales had told.
It gnawed for something lost, some word, some nest.

Their eyes were milky, wide, and pale with mold.
They blinked too slow, or not at all, or wide.
Their gestures echoed habits they once sold.

One bowed beside a mailbox and just cried.
One knelt and scraped the earth as if to pray.
One hummed a song and waited for a guide.

A teacher still would write the empty day
upon a wall with blood from faded hand.
Her students watched, but knew not how to stay.

They did not chase unless you dared to stand.
They walked as if the world had left them numb.
They circled ruins as if under command.

Their mouths, forever parted, did not hum
they whispered through the bones of ruined dogs.
They mouthed the names of children, mothers, some

who may have lived before the breath turned to fog.
I watched one trace a doorframe with her face.
She wept without her tears, a girl still in clogs.

And in their midst, I found no greed, no race
no armies, borders, flags, or prideful claims.
Just need. Just thirst. Just time without a place.

A man with only half a face drew names
in ash, then sat, as if to beg or wait.
Another chewed a crucifix in flames.

A dancer limped her final practiced gait.
She twirled with broken limbs but did not fall.
Her body mimed a grace too old for hate.

They did not growl. They barely groaned at all.
They walked like sleep had pulled the mind away.
Their silence filled the corners of each hall.

Some had no limbs, yet crawled as if to pray.
Some clutched at air, at nothing, at a sigh.
Some stared as if already in the clay.

I watched them once beneath a carbon sky.
They circled an old man who could not flee.
They did not bite. Just moaned and passed him by.

Perhaps they sought what we could never be
not meat or muscle, not revenge or fire
but proof that pain can still recall the sea.

One pinned a drawing to a barbed wire spire:
a house, a tree, a smile, a distant bell.
She dropped her head and did not cross the wire.

I stood and wrote while wind began to swell.
Their forms were framed in dusk like tragic art.
I felt no hate, no fear I had to quell.

And true to form, stubborn with my part,
began to hum a line I thought was dead.
It left my lips. It reached a thing with heart.

The corpse turned once, then bowed its fractured head.
It did not chase. It did not shriek or glee.
It vanished with the night, with none to dread.

I thought they'd chase. I thought they'd tear and bite.
Instead they mourned, and vanished into night.

No hunger like any the stories ever told
just memory that rots but won't release its hold.

They did not growl. They hummed as if in prayer.
And still I wrote, though none were left to care.

Their eyes were glass. Their hands recalled a door.
They moved through towns we never see no more.

And me? I watched the one who did not kill
a girl who sang, and made the dusk go still.

I cannot say if death forgets its own.
But some return, and hum, and stand alone.

The Shivering Girl

She stood beside the playground gate,
her dress was torn and red.
A teacup dangled from one hand,
the other dripped instead.

Her hair was full of ribboned knots,
her socks hung at her knees.
She sang a tune with broken parts
too soft to catch the keys.

"Come play," she said, and no one moved.
"Come see what I can do."
Her voice was sweet and didn't shake.
Her shadow split in two.

She walked but didn't make a sound,
her mouth a curling hum.
Her tongue was black, her eyes were gray,
her lullaby undone.

A brother tried to bring her home.
A neighbor reached to help.
Her mother screamed into her hands
and never called for help.

The playground rusted overnight.
The swing still rocked its chain.
And every dusk, a child appears
to hum that song again.

Lights blink in the store.
A mother grabs canned peaches
and forgets her list.

The swing still moving
no children in the schoolyard.
A bird lands, then leaves.

A child just stands there.
No coat. No shoes. No blinking.
No one asks her name.

The Boy Beneath the Steps

He hid beneath the wooden steps
behind the neighbor's shed.
He watched her hum, and did not breathe.
He bit his hand instead.

His mother searched with open arms,
her voice too sharp to hear.
The boy just stared and counted slow
the numbers felt like years.

They found him when the light returned,
eyes wide, but gaze not whole.
He whispered, "She was singing still
and something took my soul."

They laughed that day, though something smelled like smoke.
A child went still, and no one dared to joke.

The birds were wrong. Their wings cut sharp, not wide.
I saw one land. I watched its eye decide.

The news said, "Stay inside and stay prepared."
But fear, at first, still sounded like a dare.

So I took notes, while others made their plans.
I wrote the fall down softly; held it in my hands.

A woman coughed. A man said, "It's just dust."
The silence after sharpened every rust.

The stores stayed open. Sales were never slow.
But no one asked how fast the weeds could grow.

The clocks still worked. The radios still played.
But something underneath had just decayed.

I stayed unseen. I watched them play pretend.
I think I knew then; how this would end.

Subject I: Day Three

My name is Michael…

I think it still is.
I've been writing this on my arm,
over and over.

It's not blood yet. It's still ink.

I keep forgetting
the sound of my own voice,
so I say my name out loud:
Michael.

Sometimes it sounds like
someone else's name.

There's a ringing in my bones,
not my ears, my bones.
Like a tuning fork buried under skin.

I thought maybe it was just fever.
But fever doesn't make you crave…
things

I saw my shadow
and didn't recognize
the way it moved.
It tilted its head before I did.
It smiled first.

If you find this,

don't try to help me.

Just remember that I tried not to forget.

And if I turn,

don't believe I meant it.

Intersection

The traffic lights blinked out of sync.
A bus stalled at the bridge
and no one honked.

Pigeons circled once,
then vanished.

A man in a suit began to run.
He didn't stop at the crosswalk.

The street vendors left
their grills still burning.
Smoke rose for hours,
seasoning the air with something
that was not meat.

<u>Broadcast: Error 13</u>

...hospitalized in clusters now...
                        "That's not live, is it?"

...we urge calm and continued...
                        "They always say to stay calm.
                        That means it's bad."

sources confirm that in Sector 7 there are reports of...

...this is a clip from earlier...

the child appears to be...
                        "She's not moving. Should she be moving?"

...authorities are not using the word... not yet.
                        "They're not using the word. You notice that?"
                        "Wait. Where *is* this? That looks like our street."

back to you, Julia...
                        "It's just a drill. They'd tell us if it wasn't."
                        "They' d tell us."
                        "They' d tell us."

They told us not to worry, so we tried.
They named it nothing, so we let it slide.

The screens blinked red, but we were trained to scroll.
The anchors smiled, and no one paid the toll.

One child said the siren hurt her skin.
We laughed and told her not to let it in.

The phones still rang. The toast still burned its side.
We thought that fear was something you could hide.

A cough was just a cough. We'd heard before.
The world had cried wolf once, and maybe more.

We changed the channel, checked the weather twice.
The calm was real, but laced with something ice.

We joked, then paused. Then joked a little less.
We felt the air rehearse its great undress.

The subway stalled. A voice cut off mid-speech.
We stared, as if the screen could maybe teach.

It wasn't war. No soldier took a post.
Just whispers thickening like a coastal ghost.

A siren passed. No one stood up to see.
We named it "just a drill" and let it be.

But I remember when the signal skipped
and silence took the air where voices slipped.

It wasn't then, not fully. Not just yet.
But breath began to learn what to forget.

And in that static, something leaned to speak.
We didn't run. We didn't dare feel weak.

<u>*Subject 2: Day Five*</u>

It was raining or bleeding.
I can't tell anymore.
It hits the roof the same way.

I used to write poetry
or maybe
I just liked the sound of it.

There was a dog.
She barked at the mirror.
She knew before I did.

I said goodbye to my brother
ten times.
He only heard one.

My fingers keep counting things
stairs, stars, bones.
But the numbers come in colors now.

I miss the taste of toast.
It's the little things,
like remembering you had a name.

I think my hands
are someone else's now.
They keep reaching

even when I sleep.

Canto II – Not Yet, Not Yet

It started as a cough behind a screen,
A sound dismissed, a throat too dry to care.
We laughed, then paused then changed the magazine.

The elevator doors exhaled stale air.
A man stepped out and didn't hold his phone.
A woman stared and found no reason there.

The headlines blurred, the data overgrown
with graphs and guesses, red expanding rings.
We read. We shrugged. We went to bed alone.

A dog refused to bark at passing things.
The pigeons left the church two days too soon.
The wind forgot the tune the tower sings.

We marked our days with coffee, toast, and noon.
The streets grew thin; the crowds began to shift.
A child was told to stay inside her room.

The teacher spoke with smiles that didn't lift.
The chalkboard held a date no one erased.
We called it temporary. Called it drift.

A man in gloves walked past a child, unbraced.
Their eyes did not align. The breath was wrong.
He vanished through the market, slow, un-chased.

The music store played silence in its song.
The bells above the door began to rust.
A whisper walked where voices had belonged.

A preacher raised his hand and spoke of trust.
A woman prayed through cloth upon her face.
The offerings turned dusty, then to dust.

A call went out. A doctor left his place.
A patient followed him and did not blink.
The hallway lights began to pulse in place.

The nurse said don't forget to eat or think.
Her eyes were red. Her hand stayed near her sleeve.
She smiled. Then paused. Then leaned against the sink.

A siren passed, but no one took their leave.
The fire alarm stayed quiet, which felt wrong.
The birds returned, then circled, then deceived.

A boy looked up and said it's been too long
since someone came to take him back from school.
His phone was dead. His voice was not as strong.

A woman in a coat broke every rule
she knocked and knocked, though glass was in her hair.
Her knuckles left behind a bloody jewel.

They let her in. Her breathing touched the air.
Her mouth was torn. Her eyes too wide to read.
The man beside her stepped back from the stair.

And then it came the sound beneath the need.
A howl not meant for ear or bone or wall.
A voice that wasn't voice but echo's seed.

It carried through the vents, then down the hall
It knocked on ribs. It asked to be let in.
It crawled down wires and climbed up every call.

And once it sang, we could not cage it in.
The boy who coughed was never seen again.
The nurses prayed. The preacher dropped his grin.

A crack began beneath the skin of when.
And time itself grew fragile at the edge
no longer if, no longer why, but when.

We shut the doors. We sharpened every pledge.
The air itself began to choose its side.
The night turned still. The moon began to wedge

itself inside our hearts like something tried
to keep us warm, but only found us wide.

The story cracked. The pages wouldn't bind.
The world spoke back in pieces misaligned.

A whisper here. A rusted swing that creaks.
A kettle howling things it shouldn't speak.

The news grew faint, then scattered into sound.
And voices rose from sky, and gates, and ground.

No plot remained. Just fragments in the dust.
A list half-read. A swing that wouldn't rust.

They told their truths in sugar, rhyme, and ash.
In boiled tea. In footsteps near the trash.

The dead, you see, don't rise in rows or ranks.
They hum. They tilt. They watch from over banks.

One child repeats a song with broken thread.
One woman stirs a pot she knows is dead.

A man writes prayers on post-its. Just in case.
A dog runs home, then stops outside the gate.

And me, I write not to connect the tale,
but gather sparks before the shadows pale.

Anatomy of the Dead I

The teeth remain,
though they no longer wait for bread.
Some still twitch when lullabies are near.
Some crack when names are spoken.

The tongue forgets its mother first.
It curls,
not to speak,
but to taste the memory of vowels.

Gums rot slower than regret.
A hum can last a week inside the jaw
if it began in grief.

We've found molars etched with prayers.
Whispers sealed in plaque.
One corpse bit the corner of a hymn
and still mouths Amen
when the wind comes soft.

The voice is gone.
But the mouth repeats
whatever silence left behind.

These are the echoes. These are teeth and time.
The world that fell out of sequence and rhyme.

So take these scraps. They'll guide, but not explain.
A song, a swing, a footprint in the rain.

Static

She turned the dial and heard her name,
but not in voice, not quite the same.
It crackled through the kitchen air
a whisper caught between despair
and just a broken morning game.

One window won't close.
A voice calls out from upstairs.
No one goes to check.

<u>*Internal Report*</u>

I locked the door without thinking.
Twice.

The sirens were soft.
Softer than I imagined.

My neighbor screamed something.
Not a name.
Just… something.

I made tea.

The water boiled too long,
and I didn't stop it.

The dog won't come back.
Footprints near the neighbor's gate.
Something red and soft.

Playground Games

They gathered by the yellow slide,
their laughter low and slow.
The seesaw rocked without a hand,
the sandbox held no snow.

A skipping rope lay tangled tight,
no rhythm left to keep.
They spun in circles, eyes half-closed
like children trapped in sleep.

Their song was built from hollow chords,
a rhyme no mouth should know:
"One for the crow, and two for the flame,
and three for the ones below."

A father screamed, but none looked up.
A dog turned back and ran.
The carousel spun on its own,
the sky turned white, then tan.

They're still there when the moon is full.
Their shadows don't align.
And every swing that creaks at dusk
keeps perfect, perfect time.

Green Without Permission

They came back in blades,
not banners.

Not in glory
but in crawl.

Moss took the tires first.

Ivy cradled the swings.
The merry-go-round
shrieked once,
then turned no more.

A tree grew where Lila once stood.

I remember her red scarf
now coiled in bark
like a shy thing.

No prayers were asked.
No offerings left.

No one begged the grass
to be gentle.

It was never our earth.
We were only its heat.

Now we cool.

Now it blooms.

And the
weeds
do not ask.

The Hungering Choir

They came not with a scream, but soft amen,
Through chapel doors that breathed in rust and falls,
Each footstep rang like silence pressed by ten.

I passed a corridor lined with breathing walls,
Where hymns were cracked and grey with incense flame,
Tongues stitched with prayer beads hummed in chapel stalls.

A preacher stood who'd long forgot his name,
His lips were sealed with wire, not by rule,
Yet still he mouthed a sermon just the same.

I saw a girl baptized in sacred fuel,
She smiled through teeth engraved with candle wax,
She sang in notes that scorched the churchyard pool.

Her voice awoke the pews, now black with tracks
Of crawling hands that once held rosaries,
The statues wept with tears like blistered flax.

One aisle stretched out in moaning minor keys
While lungs inflated slowly from the floor,
Exhaling fog that whispered mockeries.

A wall bore marks where dozens begged the door,
Their knuckles left in smears of bone and ink,
They chanted names no saint could still restore.

The choir rose with jaws that couldn't blink,
Their hymnals bound in skin and stitched anew,
Their chorus cracked the altar's final link.

I passed a saint with meat still clinging through
Her ribs a relic of devotion's tide,
She offered me her tongue and something true:

"Each page you write invites what we must hide.
The choir grows with every whispered word
So choose your verse with care, or walk aside."

A thurible of hair swung like a bird,
Its smoke replaced the organ's shattered lungs,
Its incense drawn from things the grave preferred.

A deacon crawled with bells tied to his tongues,
He rang beneath a stained-glass window's scream,
Each chime a warning strung from twisted rungs.

The stained glass bled. The candles fed the steam
Of flesh combusting gently into praise
The narthex pulsed with sacrificial theme.

A scroll unrolled, aflame with final days,
It bore the names of those who tried to pray
But woke to find the psalms in disarray.

The font was thick with blood that would not grey,
Still warm from those who knelt and did not rise.
The crucifix was gone, its cross astray.

And on the ceiling, arms began to rise
Not painted, real like branches in reverse
They clutched at air and reached through chapel skies.

The choir kept singing, always in one verse:
"We are the hunger that remembers grace,
We are the hymn that marks the world's last hearse."

The echoes wrapped around the pulpit's face
And drew a veil of breathless, boiling silk,
While serpents curled where kneelers left their trace.

I found a book of pages scorched like milk,
Each line was burned but still retained its scream,
It told of tongues that turned to rot and ilk.

A candle hissed beside a holy beam,
Its flame alive with eyes that dared to blink,
It whispered, "Poet, write what we redeem."

So I obeyed, with ink that dared not think,
And carved the lines on bone where blood still mourns.
And all I knew was gone in a blink

The song still moaned, though all its mouths were torn,
A hunger sung in thirds, unclosed, unblessed
They feasted not on flesh, but those unborn.

I smelled the chlorine long before the gate.
A memory preserved, but far too late.

The ticket booth still offered half-off days.
A sun-faded cartoon beamed through the haze.

The wave machine was quiet, stiff with rust.
The turnstiles moved, but only when they must.

I thought of children racing to get wet.
Now every splash is something to forget.

The lifeguard stand was empty, but not clean.
I've never feared a smile more serene.

Safety Is Our Pleasure

Welcome to the Drownery,
Where bubbles bloom like sores.
Please keep your limbs inside the pit
And never swim to shores.

The lifeguard wears his smile well
It's sewn across his face.
He hasn't blinked since '91,
But keeps a steady pace.

Our whistles blow in broken time,
Our flags are made of teeth.
We'll rescue you in order, friend
The ones who scream beneath.

You must be tall to die this ride.
No shoes. No hope. No grace.
And if you hear the trumpet call,
Don't look it in the face.

We serve refreshments twice a year
Ash-cones, bleach, and bone.
We thank you for your patronage.
Enjoy the undertone.

Don't worry if the water speaks.
It lies. It always did.
Just float. Relax. Unclench your hands.
You're safer if you've hid.

Our rules are carved in bladderwrack,
Our waivers signed in brine.
No exit here. No lifeboats left.
The water tastes like time.

So laugh! So sink! So join the show!
We welcome every guest.
Your body is our souvenir.
We'll hang it with the rest.

Safety Intermission

Thank you for your patience, guest!
We know the wait was long.
A minor leak in Sector Four
has flushed the weaker throng.

Please do not mind the warning lights
red's festive, after all.
And any limbs you didn't bring
are purely carnival.

Remember: drowning is a choice!
So choose it with a grin.
Our staff will fetch what's left of you
and guide your pieces in.

The scent of burning cartilage?
It's part of our new line!
Eau de Decomposition™,
For guests who love the brine.

Our lifeguards may be slower now
Some jaws have come unhinged.
But rest assured, their loyalty
Has only slightly thinned.

So clap along! Your screams are stars!
Your fear a prize we crave.
The intermission's almost done
Return now to your grave.

Dead Float

At Splashquake Cove where children laughed,
The slides now echo screams
Of lifeguards torn and families halved
Inside drowned daydreams.

The wave machine began to groan,
Then stilled in solemn dread,
Before it surged with moaning tones
Not water, but the dead.

Their bloated hands gripped plastic rails,
With skin like kelp and slate,
Eyes blank as rusted shower pails,
They shuffled through the gate.

One cannonballed from high above
His jawbone fell mid-flight.
Another chewed the foam of love
In a toddler's pool of fright.

A vendor's brain served à la carte,
With mustard on the side,
As zombie lifeguards tore apart
The ones who tried to hide.

The lazy river turned to red,
Its current choked with limbs,
A disembodied plastic head
Still gurgled water hymns.

The chlorine stung, it didn't cleanse,
　　The plague was in the mist.
A girl emerged with sharpened lens
　　She shot, then made a list.

But no escape. The exits sealed.
　　A bite behind the ear.
The undead party was revealed
　　Eternal summer here.

So if you hear a splashing sound
Where once the lifeguards played,
Remember: even water drowns
When dead things want to wade.

The laughter lingered long after the blood.
The water stank of chlorine, salt, and mud.

The colors blurred. The speakers barked a song.
I ran. I wrote. I waited far too long.

A float went by with something in its grin.
A plastic crown. A jaw. A bit of skin.

And still I watched; not brave, not even sure.
Just scribbling proof that horror isn't pure.

The carnival decayed beneath its scream.
I held a pen as if to pinch the dream.

But then the red arrived in finer thread
a whisper smeared across a child's bed.

Not blood that splashed, but softly stayed.
A handprint where no hand had ever played.

The scream gave way to coughing in the dark.
The red was not a howl, but just a mark.

It clung to knobs. It trailed behind a sigh.
It paused in doorways. Waited to reply.

And me I left the funhouse far behind.
What followed next was grief, not fear, not mind.

The red returned. Not vivid, but precise.
It tasted more like silence than like vice.

Subject 3: Unknown

Name?
No.
No.
My name

Was…

was room.
No.
Blue chair.
Chair…

laugh?
She… she
said "stay."
I didn't.

Laugh.
Or scream.

Or sun?
Was sun.
What is sun?

My name?

The Red Was Never Meant to Stay

The red was never meant to stay this long.
A cough, a door ajar, a mother's cry.
We told ourselves the silence wasn't wrong.

A siren whispered low, then screamed its song.
The birds flew off. The dogs forgot to lie.
The red was never meant to stay this long.

The fever lit the hallway swift and strong.
A handprint bloomed across the window's eye.
We told ourselves the silence wasn't wrong.

The school dismissed too late. The lines grew long.
The girl at aisle four began to die.
The red was never meant to stay this long.

The news broke teeth on what it couldn't mong
the footage blurred, the anchors failed to try.
We told ourselves the silence wasn't wrong.

It smeared the doorknobs, hummed inside the song.
It bled the day beneath a burning sky.
The red was never meant to stay this long.
We told ourselves the silence wasn't wrong.

Some stayed and died. Some stayed and turned to air.
But others moved too lost to name their despair.

They carried bricks that once held a wall.
They whispered names and didn't speak at all.

I saw them walk with pockets full of thread.
They knotted prayers to mark the halfway dead.

A man once stopped to fix a broken shoe.
He said, "I walk for those who never knew."

They didn't call it hope. They knew that lie.
They carried rope instead and watched the sky.

Some bartered light. Some traded food for sound.
Some left their maps in pieces on the ground.

A child gave me chalk and said, "Draw home."
Then vanished through a field of plastic foam.

And I didn't ask them where or why.
I only walked. I let their silence cry.

They moved like songs and the world forgot to hum.
They moved like breath still learning not to come.

The Ones Who Fled

The living fled, but had no place to go.
The maps were wrong. The names no longer fit.
They followed roads that vanished under snow.

Each mile they walked erased the thought of "it"
the life before, the dailiness they wore.
They bartered food for warmth, for shoes, for grit.

A woman wore old keys like sacred lore.
She claimed they opened every kind of gate.
Her fingers bled. She touched the ground and swore.

A man repaired a truck then sealed his fate
it ran one hour, then died beside a barn.
He left a note that read, "Just past too late."

A child slept wrapped in a coat of yarn.
Her brother kept a lighter in his sock.
He said, "The flame must never come to harm."

One group moved fast, like fugitives on clock.
They slept in stints of five and took no sound.
Their rules were harsh: don't pray, don't beg, don't knock.

They left no fire, no prints upon the ground.
They called their tent "a little bit of brave."
Their names were signs they never passed around.

One girl survived inside a flooded cave.
She learned to catch the fish that feared the light.
She kept a journal on a stone she'd shave.

A boy lived weeks with just a plastic kite.
He wrote old poems on it with a pin.
He said, "It helps to hold something in flight."

Some wandered north and vanished in the wind.
Some stayed and painted flames upon their doors.
Some taught the trees to carry sound again.

A mother marked the days with grains and spores.
She told her son, "This one is for your laugh."
She stored each laugh in jars beside her chores.

They did not lead with grief, or dream, or staff.
They walked with rhythm only loss could keep.
They broke their bread, then drew a shared epitaph.

And I, alone, too tired to cry or sleep,
walked west through wreckage, seeking some old street.
I found a doll half-buried, sunk too deep.

I sat and watched the moon no longer sweet,
just pale and distant, like a closing eye.
I whispered rhymes to hold my failing feet.

I met a group who chose to never lie.
They told their wounds in poems and in sweat.
They left behind no corpse without a cry.

One told me, "Every day I choose regret,
but still I walk. I plant where I have lost."
They planted weeds, and named each one a debt.

Another carried nails, not to accost
but build. He hammered crates into a raft.
He said, "We float until we pay the cost."

I watched a girl draw maps in paper craft.
She folded streets and turned them into sails.
She launched a fleet of hopes into the draft.

I met a boy whose memory always fails.
Each day he asked, "Is this the end or start?"
I gave him poems he fed them to the gales.

And me? I wrote, though breaking was an art.
I wrote their feet, their fires, their silent code.
I wrote them whole, not cracked or torn apart.

The Cracks

The floor split

on a Tuesday.

No one saw.

No boots were there

to echo on tile,

no mothers around

to curse the draft.

Just silence,

then lichen.

It came first as moisture,

then green,

then greener.

A fern unfurled in the hallway

where someone once whispered love.

Moss stitched over the gunfire.

We wrote on walls to be remembered.

Now the walls are soft.

The ivy climbs
like it's searching for someone to hold.

But it doesn't need us.

The cracks are doors,
and the earth does not knock.

The Break

The signals stopped mid-sentence.
Elevators froze with people inside.
A child tried to call her father.
The line clicked once.
Then nothing.

Every sound afterward
felt like a question
we no longer had the language to answer.

The Seed

It didn't ask to fall
the seed.

It rode the wind
like everything else:

It found the mouth of a soldier,
open in sleep or death.
Nestled in the wet dark.
Waited.

The body did not reject it.
It rooted
where words once lived.

Days passed like animals.
Quiet and hungry.

Then the mouth bloomed.
Petals where teeth had been.

The seed did not ask.
The seed did not care.

It was only doing
what it was made for.

When the Sound Changed

The pigeons left before the sirens came.
A mother said, don't touch your eyes or mouth.
The news went static, but the sky looked tame.
A child drew teeth inside a paper house.

A mother said, don't touch your eyes or mouth.
The dog refused to bark, just stared instead.
A child drew teeth inside a paper house.
The preacher whispered, something's wrong with bread.

The dog refused to bark, just stared instead.
The phones rang once, then never made a sound.
The preacher whispered, something's wrong with bread.
A cough was heard but didn't draw a crowd.

The phones rang once, then never made a sound.
A scream came late, then echoed down the drain.
A cough was heard but didn't draw a crowd.
The air grew thick. The birds did not explain.

A scream came late, then echoed down the drain.
The news went static, but the sky looked tame.
The air grew thick. The birds did not explain.
The pigeons left before the sirens came

I found this tucked beneath a rusted frame
burnt down one side, the other warped by flame.

The ink had fled, as if it tried to hide
before I came, before the truth had died.

I can't be sure what they had meant to say.
The meaning, like their bodies, slipped away.

But I have learned the way each silence bends.
I know how this begins. And how it ends.

Internal Transmission #471-C (Partial Recovery)

Patient intake exceeded projected ████████████████
████████████████ Please advise all staff to ████████
██
██████ Containment protocol █████████████████████
██
Visitors restricted to ████████ do not approach ████
██
████ we are not equipped for ████████ the child in Room
████████████████████████████ bit through ████████
████████████████ code black ████████ reassigned to █
█ no confirmation ████████████ no cure ██████████
████████ don't ██████████████████████████████
████████████████████████ don't ████████████████
████████████ don't look ████████████████

City Without Pause

I reached the edge where towers touched no sky.
Their windows wept in mirrored shades of blue.
Their doors hung slack, like mouths too dry to cry.

The pavement cracked where weeds had broken through.
The crosswalks flashed commands in silent beat
"Walk Wait Walk Wait" though none obeyed or knew.

A billboard screamed: You're More Than Just a Seat!
Its paint was peeled, its promise out of date.
Below it lay the bones of old deceit.

The subways moaned, though empty, still they wait.
Their tunnels echoed scraps of distant trains.
The air was filled with static, dust, and fate.

A stairwell buzzed with looping soft refrains
a jingle from a snack no one still eats.
It played between old fire alarms and stains.

One speaker cracked and begged to scan receipts.
Another coughed out weather from last May.
Each sound became a chorus in repeats.

The churches had no priests, but still would play
recordings of confessions in the dark.
A whisper said, "Forgive me," then would fray.

A mall declared: Our Sale Begins at Park!
It echoed up and down the broken tiles.
Its mannequins were cracked and posed and stark.

Inside a bank, the vaults had lost their files.
A screen still blinked: Your Balance Is Declined.
The lights above gave off fluorescent smiles.

I wandered where the memories were mined
not gold, but voice, and image, and regret.
A message read: Please speak your need. Be kind.

I pressed one button, just to see the net.
It printed out a ticket with no name.
It read: Your past is not recoverable yet.

Each floor was filled with silence that became
a kind of song of data, loss, and dust.
One hallway sang the anthem of a game.

A food court played old jazz through wires and rust.
The chairs were gone. The menus blinked goodbye.
A straw dispenser fell apart with trust.

In glass I saw my face, and heard a cry
replayed in echo from an upper floor.
It said my name but softer than the sky.

One elevator hummed an endless score
and opened, though I pressed no button in.
I stepped inside and pressed a single door.

It took me nowhere. Just a voice began:
The journey up is closed. The path below
requires your grief to map where you began.

I stepped back out. The air began to grow
chimes from phones that hadn't rung in years.
Their screens lit up with names I didn't know.

In one old theatre, with rows like tears,
the film still played a loop of someone's hands
tying a shoe, then fading into smears.

The hands like my father's, soft and tanned.
I watched them move, then vanish with a glitch.
The film reversed. The voice said, "Understand."

And I, the poet, stood inside the pitch
of echoes, where the human trace remains
not full, not true, but still a voice to stitch.

What Grows Without Asking

They said the city was dead. But dead things don't twitch.
Dead things don't hum.

The first time I noticed, it was small
a hairline crack in the pavement
where the grocery used to be.
I passed it every day, but one morning it was wider.
Deeper.

And green.
Not a soft green, not new-life green.
A green that waited.

I told myself it was moss, just moss.

That's how it always starts.
But then came the buds. Not from trees.
From bone.

I saw a ribcage nestled in a burned-out bus
split wide open like a cradle, and something had taken root.
Not just one stalk, but many. Pale stems spiraling upward,
almost tender.
I didn't stay to look for a face.

Later, I found a daffodil blooming from a skull.
Not planted.
Not arranged.
Just there.

Yellow as sunlight I don't remember.

The vines crawl along ceiling beams now.
They thread through empty sockets, weave cradles in abandoned windows.
There are no birds. Still, the nests grow full.

No one planted these things.
There is no gardener.
No rain.
Still, they reach.

Sometimes, beneath the floorboards,
I swear I hear a breath.
Not mine. Not wind.
Something lower. Older.
A root remembering how to speak.

I don't touch the green anymore.
It touches back.

The Bloomers

They said it started
in the skin.
Not a rash.
Not heat.
Just a pulse
beneath the pulse.

Veins forgot their maps.
Bones began to hum.
One woman claimed
she tasted bark
instead of bread.

They didn't die,
not first.
They walked in loops
around parking lots,
whispering the names
of flowers
they'd never seen.

Then came the blooming.

Lips split

not with screams,
but petals
wet and pink,
and far too many.

Fingernails curled back
to reveal
seeds.

Their spines grew moss.

One boy,
barefoot in the street,
left mushrooms
where he stepped.

They sang,
but never the same song.

Each voice
a garden of its own.

We burned the first group.
Ash stuck like spring

But the bloomers
do not stay burned.
They reassemble
in the shade
like roots
remembering
where a throat once was.

They don't want meat.
They want breath.

So they can plant
what comes next.

And now,
when someone itches
beneath the jaw,
we don't ask.
We cut.

And if it bleeds green
we run.

They bloom, yes
but what grows is hunger,
not grace.
Not flowers.

Just the echo of once-hands,
once-names,
turned fragrant
with forgetting.

The Garden Remembers Blood

The flowers here do not grow toward light.
They grow toward heat.
Toward bone.

The garden is lush, yes
but it is not kind.

Every petal leans into rot.
Every root tastes of copper.

I knelt once, to smell a bloom the color of bruises.
It opened for me. Not like a kiss,
but a wound.

There are blossoms shaped like screams.
Ferns that hiss when touched.

The vines remember necks.
The soil remembers wrists.

We buried too much here
thinking it would stay quiet.

But the garden keeps a ledger.
And every spring,
it adds another name
in pollen.

If dead things spoke, they'd not use mouths or sound.
They'd speak through shoes left waiting on the ground

Through lullabies that never reached their ends,
through open doors, through letters never sent.

I tried to turn away, to close the page,
but silence presses louder than rage.

Their voices bloom between the written word
not to be mourned, just to be heard.

We Are the Quiet That Came Too Late

we speak as one
we are the quiet that came too late.

we are the dust behind your lungs.
we are the lull in your sirens.
we are the static between your prayers.

we are not rage.
rage burns too fast.

we are the hush after.

after the headline,
after the screaming,

after the lights blinked and did not return.

we are not the dark.
we are what walks inside it.

you called us plague.
you called us rot.
but we were once children
with grapes in our hands.
we were once names.

we remember breath.
we remember needing.
we do not miss it.

we were made by your forgetting.

you did not look up.
you did not close the door.
you did not check the child twice.

you said:
not here. not yet. not us.

and so we came.

We watched your hands grow clean with fear.
We learned your screens could lie.
We opened locks you thought forgot
with only memory and time.

we are the door without hinges.
we are the meal without a plate.
we are the voice that hums your lullabies
in a language your tongue has not earned.

one of us
still wears her ballet shoes.
one of us
hums through a broken tooth.
one of us
cannot stop turning the doorknob.
one of us
has your brother's laugh.
one of us is already in your house.

we know your scent.
we know the quietest path to your bed.

you dream of birds.
we eat the feathers.

we do not hunger.
we remember hunger.

do not ask why we do not speak.
We speak now.

do not ask what we want.
we want nothing.
that is why we never stop.

we are your neighbor's soft footsteps.
we are the knock you almost heard.
we are the shape
your dog won't look at.
we are the scream
beneath your dream.

you had prayers.
you forgot to bury them.
we are not your end.
we are what your end becomes.

we are the quiet that came too late.
and we have never left.

Elegy in Circles

I found a field where none would plant or plow.
The grass was black with soot, the soil warm.
A circle walked it, slow and unknowing how.

They groaned not hate, but hunger made to swarm.
Their mouths ajar, their jaws unsure, unplaced.
They moved as if rehearsing one last form.

A child among them wore a mask untraced.
Its eyes were coins, its cheeks smeared red with oil.
It turned and paused, as if it once embraced.

I did not run. I stepped onto their coil.
They parted slow, like wind does through a fire.
No teeth were shown. No limbs were raised to spoil.

One brushed my coat. Another, with desire,
seemed almost to remember how to kneel.
Their hands were twitching shapes that could inspire.

A man among them dragged a spinning wheel
perhaps he'd once been tailor, now remade.
He groaned a tune no longer meant to heal.

A woman wore her veil as if a blade
had not yet kissed her fully into rot.
She traced a name into the dust and stayed.

A group sat down as if they'd once been taught
to picnic, learn, or speak of things to come.
They stared at sky with longing tightly caught.

One lifted what was once a faded drum
and patted it with bones in halting pace.
The sound was soft. It echoed like a hum.

I saw no rage, no battle in their face
just loss unfiltered, staring without ask.
Their horror was the slowness of their grace.

A boy still gripped a tattered science mask.
He blinked, then blinked again, then stood in still.
He turned away and vanished in the dusk.

I left no trap. I left no urge to kill.
I only wrote what I could safely feel:
They live, but not the way we once held will

They shuffled past a graveyard grown in teal.
The moss had climbed the names into a blur.
The turned stepped round each stone as if still real.

I followed one into a house of fur
its walls were pelts, its floor made up of glass.
He stopped beside a picture, then demurred.

The picture bore a face perhaps from class,
a child's grin with teeth too wide, too wild.
He touched it once, then vanished through the mass.

A woman turned, and though her face defiled
with scars and bites, her eyes met mine with calm.
She did not speak. Her stare was clear, unstyled.

I whispered verse beneath a cracked old psalm
just fragments of a lullaby once known:
The stars are tired, but you are still the balm.

I placed a page beside a weathered bone
that bore a bracelet etched with letters faint.
It read: Dear Eli. Bring your sister home.

A man walked past with movements slow and quaint.
He did not moan, but breathed in shallow rhyme.
His pace had weight, as if he'd once been paint.

And I, the poet, standing out of time,
knew they were not what tales had made them seem.
They did not curse. They did not climb.

They simply mourned the silence of the stream.
Their lives were caught between decay and dust
not evil, just the end of someone's dream.

The Soil's Memory

The soil never asks.
It only takes.

Rain. Ash. Bone.
The names we whispered while we dug.

It does not weep.
But it keeps.

I pressed my hand
to the earth once,
where a girl had been laid
with her favorite book and her last breath.

The dirt was warm.
It hummed.

Not a song
something even older.

The roots moved beneath my palm,
slow and deliberate.

I think they were remembering her.
I think they remembered us all.

Even the things we meant to hide.
Especially those.

Still Warm

We heard the knock.
Three short. Two long.
Just like we taught her.

No one moved.
The radio was dead.
The soup had gone cold
but we still stirred it.

Another knock.
Same rhythm.
Same pause between.

She never made it back from school.
We had checked
the hospitals,
the streets,
the rows of shoes by the fence.

We told ourselves
someone else taught the code.
Maybe a survivor.
Maybe a trick.

Maybe.

I said don't open it.
I said wait until morning.
I said

The latch turned anyway.

No scream.
No figure.
No sound
but air
that didn't belong.

There was only a shoe.
Yellow.
Velcro strap torn.
Still warm.

The door won't close now.
It creaks at night.
It clicks the code.

Three short.
Two long.
Wait.

Litany of the Failed Turning

We were almost light.
We were almost last.
We were the ones who staggered too slow from the blast.

We heard the prayer, but not the end.
We felt the cure, but not the mend.

Our names were spoken once too soft, too late.
We rose in silence, mouths still full of fate.

We wore our bodies like borrowed coats.
We sang our hunger in unpitched notes.

The walking was the price we paid.
Not for death
but for simply being afraid.

One step. One breath. One step. No more.
We circled what we could not restore.

There were songs.
We remember the rhythm, not the words.
There were bells.
We remember the toll, not the reason.

We are the hymn that ends before the chord.
We are the echo in the room without a lord.

Do not pity us.
Do not praise.
Only walk
onward through the maze.

The turning was not failed,
it was refused.
We are the ones the world confused.

Dust in our throat.
Soil in our sleep.
We walk the circle the living keep.

Noise Has Memory Too

Once, the city had a rhythm.
Not a song,
no, songs are too clean.

It was messier than that.
A blur of taxi brakes and
children shrieking for ice cream,
a man on a corner radio shouting
"Twenty-four, twenty-four, get it while it's hot!"
and all of it overlapping, crashing,

alive.

I used to think it was chaos.
But it was a kind of music.
A music that didn't need me to love it to go on.

And then the brakes stopped.
The ice cream truck didn't come back.
The man on the corner went silent so long
I forgot his voice had ever been real.

And something else
stepped into the break
between the noise.

At first, I thought it was silence.
But silence doesn't hum like that.

Doesn't tap its fingers against the glass.
Doesn't murmur through walls like it remembers
how doors work.

Now I know
the sound we called silence
is just the dead
learning how to sing.

They hum in radio static.
They echo in crosswalk tones that still blink,
though no one crosses.
They beat in the hollow of old footsteps.

When I hold my breath,
I can still hear it:

the city,
still moving

but nothing alive is making the noise.

Second Root

We thought the dead were finished.
But the soil doesn't believe in endings.

Beneath the graveyard fence,
a sprout broke loose
too soft to mourn,
too green to forget.

It twisted like a question.
Reached without eyes.

I watched it bend toward the rust of a shovel.
Toward marrow in the dirt.

Some roots seek water.
Others seek memory.

This one found her name
spelled in bone.

I do not know what grew from it.
Only that it grew.

A second root.
A second story.
Not hers,
but not not hers either.

The ground does not ask permission.
It simply rewrites.

Effective Immediately

The bulletin read:
Effective immediately, all gatherings are discouraged.
Then it read:
Effective immediately, no gatherings are allowed.
Then:
Effective immediately, no language will be used for gathering.
Then:
Effective immediately, no language will be used.
No one tore it down.
It disappeared.

Canto III – Signal Error

The power blinked, then held, then failed again.
The radios went mute without a click.
A nurse wrote names in pencil, not in pen.

The governor had once looked tall and quick
now hunched above a desk of wrinkled maps.
His speech, half-read, then swallowed by the static.

The phones rang once. Then once again. Then lapse.
A printer spat the same form on repeat.
A door was propped with boots and gauze and scraps.

A patient grinned and leaned against the heat
of someone else's silence, not their skin.
The halls smelled strange. The water wasn't sweet.

The news came late, a loop of might-have-been,
one anchor blinking slower than her cue.
The screen behind her flickered, froze, grew thin.

The mayor spoke. His tie was navy blue.
His hands shook once. His voice was clean, rehearsed.
Behind him, someone left mid-sentence through

a door that wouldn't shut. The crowd dispersed
before he finished naming what was lost.
He turned. He paused. He looked rehearsed, reversed.

The hospital was quiet. Not exhaust
not panic. Just the sound of things not moved.
A cart unrolled. A tray held jelly, glossed.

A boy sat up. His eyes were not improved.
He asked for mom. The nurse could only nod.
His voice returned, but none of it was proved.

The cameras blinked. The power lines were clawed
by storms that had no name, no maps, no eye.
A broadcast ran with no one left to laud.

The helpline played a hymn, then cut the tie.
A man confessed he never learned to shoot.
A woman laughed and whispered, nor did I.

The doorbell rang. The speaker looped reboot.
A window shattered three blocks from a scream.
A cat came home. It carried something mute.

The rooftops turned to prayer and vapored steam.
The zipline over school was wrapped in tape.
The bell rang once. The hallways felt a seam.

A teacher spoke of exit plans and shape
a code of colors, followed to the stair.
A child asked, Which color means escape?

The answer came too late. Or wasn't there.
The hallway lights went out. A girl stood still.
The air became a question no one shared.

The preacher told the radio, God will
then vanished mid-transmission, line gone dead.
The cross out front leaned slightly from the hill.

A doctor left a note beside a bed:
System nonresponsive. Patient calm.
The sheet was warm. The pillow held a head.

The fire station rang without alarm.
The trucks were parked, the boots were standing tall.
The chalkboard said: Evac begins at dawn.

At dawn, the lobby echoed with a call
just wind against the safety glass and trees.
Just quiet like a glove before the fall.

The janitor refused to take his keys.
He said, There's no one left to lock inside.
Then whistled something sad in minor E's.

The sirens sighed. The papers tried to guide.
The rules were pinned to corkboard, half askew.
A boy erased the word that said abide.

A meeting started late. The seats were few.
The man in charge had nothing left to chart.
He wiped his eyes. Then asked, Is this still true?

A mother boiled water, called it art.
Her daughter poured it slowly on the floor.
They watched the steam rise; as if nothing fell apart.

A classroom still arranged like days before
except the door was missing from its frame.
A note: All systems down. Expect no more.

The echo came again, but not by name.
It wasn't howl. It wasn't yet command.
It wasn't rage. It wasn't quite a claim.

It was the sound that says, No one's in hand.
It was the breath that orders never make.
It spread like thought too slow to understand.

And I watched the moment split and shake,
how even breaking waits before it breaks.

What The Silence Left

I did not choose to survive.
Ash settled soft on every bone.
I stayed a breath longer than the silence.
The house still hummed in ghosted chords.

Ash settled soft on every bone
a cradle where the fire dared not reach.
The house still hummed in ghosted chords,
each note a thread that would not break.

A cradle where the fire dared not reach,
my name scorched quiet in the beams.
Each note a thread that would not break
grief braided into the grain of things.

My name scorched quiet in the beams.
I stayed a breath longer than the silence.
Grief braided into the grain of things.
I did not choose to survive.

The towers fell, the wires split their threads,
but poems stay where even fire treads.

The news grew teeth and vanished in a blur,
but I still write. I still remember her.

The rules dissolved like ink in poisoned rain.
I watched the silence sharpen into strain.

But still I traced the shape of every sound,
what tried, and failed, to stay underground.

I have no flag, no anthem to repeat,
just lines that walk beside my aching feet.

The world forgot its name. It changed its face.
So I inscribed the gaps it can't replace.

I write not just to say that I was here,
but so these bones might be heard, though unclear

just distant, cracked, and echoing through flame:
a ghost of thought that never asked for fame.

The Anatomy of the Dead II

We cut the chest
and found no pulse
but warmth,
a kind that knows
it once meant mercy.

The left ventricle beat once
when a child's name was read aloud.

There are chambers filled with dust
but no collapse.
They do not love,

but they remember
how it used to start:
a hand,
a fever,
the mistake of staying.

The arteries are prayerless.
The valves echo like doors
that no longer lock.

Still, they lean toward heat
not for comfort,
but because once,
love and fire
meant the same thing.

don't

forget

to

breathe

We Spoke Until the Black Took Sound

We spoke until the black took sound away.
The power cut, and with it, every name.
Our voices flickered, bled, and slipped to gray.

A doctor tried to warn. His screen turned clay.
The city hummed, then stuttered into shame.
We spoke until the black took sound away.

The towers died like bones set out to pray.
Each blinking red collapsed into the same.
Our voices flickered, bled, and slipped to gray.

The air grew thick with wires left in fray.
The news went mute. The airwaves lost their aim.
We spoke until the black took sound away.

The hospitals forgot which child had stayed.
The lights went out. The machines called no name.
Our voices flickered, bled, and slipped to gray.

We typed "I'm here" the screen refused to say.
The silence answered all, and none to blame.
We spoke until the black took sound away.
Our voices flickered, bled, and slipped to gray.

The last voice cracked, but left a breath behind.
I held it in my chest and made it mine.

No signal left. No power line could bear
the weight of names still echoing the air.

The black took sound, but could not take the beat
that lives in wrists, or humming through our feet.

So now I write not loud, but just to prove
a voice remains where silence dared to move.

I do not shout. There's no one left to hear.
I only trace what once was said, still near.

The dead have spoken. Now the dark holds sway.
But still this pen remembers what we'd say.

Let this be stitched into the threadless light.
A line that hums when nothing else feels right.

A voice is gone. The breath remains, unwound.
We spoke. We broke. And still, I write the sound.

Origins Unnamed

We asked what began it.
We asked until our mouths cracked.

Some answered in numbers,
some in riddles,
some in prayers.

None agreed.
All were certain.

We gathered their voices anyway
not to know, but to remember
what it felt like to ask.

<u>*Transcript Fragment I*</u> <u>*"The Scientist"*</u>

(Voice Print: Dr. Mira Tanaka, Virologist, Echo Ridge Research Facility)

I thought it was fungal at first.

The way it clung to warmth, avoided light,
preferred breath held longer than lungs allow.
Ahat spoke of spores.

But spores don't remember.

And this thing
it remembered.

We mapped the genome on Day Three.
It spelled nothing we'd seen,
but the base pairs hummed when the power flickered,
like a voice under the floorboards.

I injected mice.
They sang.

I wore three layers of gloves
and still felt something trace my pulse backwards.

My assistant, Halim,
said it didn't spread
it chose.

I said that wasn't scientific.

He said neither is this kind of silence.

On Day Eight, the readings spelled out a word
in error code:

NAME ME

I deleted the file.
But it came back.

It always comes back.

(End fragment. Signal drop. No further data from Echo Ridge.)

She spoke of spores, of silent spread,
Of living mold and walking dead.

Her voice was cracked, her hands were still
The kind of calm that comes with will.

But rot remembers how to climb.
And even petri glass keeps time.

I took her notes. They smelled like rain.
Her final graph was shaped like pain.

I do not know what spores can teach.
But fungus thrives where we don't reach.

Transcript Fragment II "The Preacher"

(Voice Print: Brother Simeon Elijah, Street Prophet – 12th & Ash, South Tower Ruins)

God blinked.

That's all.
That's the whole cause.

You want science.
You want your -ologies and your carbon codes.
But I saw it
that instant when heaven looked away.

Not wrath.
Not judgment.
Just absence.

And into that holy pause,
something else stepped in.

It wasn't the devil.
He at least has rules.
This was older than sin.
Younger than mercy.

I watched a woman
kiss her daughter
and forget
the sound her name made.

I watched a man feed his brother
to the silence,
thinking it would buy him sleep.

I saw a boy
pray to the ceiling fan
because he thought it was God.

They say it came from
the sky.
I say: no.

It came from the space between words
where breath forgets
to mean something.

And when it came,
it did not ask.
It unwrote
what we meant by love.

So don't ask for cure.
Don't ask for origin.

Just know this:
The second we stopped naming one another,
the graves began to hum.

(Signal undetectable. End of audio.)

He wore a coat of soot and breath,
And named the fire more kind than death.

He said that heaven looked away
Not wrath, but God forgot to stay.

I feared his tone. I feared his grace.
I feared how ashes framed his face.

If faith is flame, then doubt is coal.
And silence needs no hymns to hold a soul.

Transcript Fragment III "The Theorist"

(Voice Print: Dr. Ezra Kale, Cognitive Meta-Systems Division, Boreal Core)

It wasn't biological.

That's where everyone went wrong.
They kept looking in blood, in bone,
in petri dishes
but this thing wasn't in the body.

It was in language.

I believe it began as a phrase,
passed like a meme,
small enough to hide in metaphor.

A sentence.
A sentence with no subject.

Like:
"It's already inside."

I traced speech patterns from outbreak zones.
I found repetition.
Words looping back, echoing in ways
that broke syntax before they broke skin.

One patient spoke in perfect reverse.
Not gibberish
actual reversal.

She said:
"You mustn't remember my name."

Then her eyes vanished.

Not closed. Not burned.
Just gone.

We ran brain scans.
Showed normal function,
except where the concept of "self" should have been
there was static.

I ran models.
Fed the data into the poetic engines.
One spat out a stanza:

"We do not catch the silence.
The silence catches us."

I laughed.
Then I cried.

Then I stopped using pronouns.

Just in case.

(Transmission corrupted. Syntax looped. Logging terminated by remote failsafe.)

She said it started with a phrase,
A word that cracked the mind like glaze.

Her charts were poems. Her labs were dark.
I saw the ghost in every spark.

If sound can break what time forgets,
Then prayers and curses share regrets.

Transcript Fragment 4 "The Skeptic"

(Voice Print: Unknown Male - Unverified Origin, Possibly Echo Zone Outlier 07)

There was no apocalypse.

That's just the name people gave the dark when the lights went out.

Look around.
No crater.
No mushroom cloud.
Just… bad weather and rumors.

You ever seen a zombie?
No, don't tell me stories. I mean *seen*.
Close enough to smell breath.

I haven't.

I saw people acting strange.
Sure.
But grief looks like madness if you're outside it.

I saw a woman burn her books. They said it was the infection.
I said maybe she was just done reading stories where no one makes it.

My neighbor buried his wife in the kitchen.
Why?
Said she asked him to.

Is that plague? Or is that love losing its balance?

All I know is:
One day they told us not to leave our homes.
The next, they stopped telling us anything.

After that, people filled in the gaps with fear.
And then poets showed up.

I think maybe that's the real infection:
the need to make a metaphor out of something that just… broke.

(Interviewer's note appended: "Subject refused to verify origin. Final remark redacted from public transcript.")

He laughed at fire, at plague, at name.
He said we conjured fear and flame.

But doubt is still a kind of creed,
And even he confessed a need.

He said we lied, that none had died.
Yet something in his voice had cried.

If metaphors are masks for pain,
Then who survives when none remain?

Transcript Fragment 5 "The Dreamer"

(Voice Print: Lina Voss, Civilian - Found in Black Wing Refuge, Window District)

I dreamed it before it began.

I remember because the sky wasn't broken yet,
but the light already flickered.

I saw a door in a field where no building had ever stood.
Just the frame,
no hinges, no knob
and wind pulling at it like it owed something.

I walked through.

Inside:

A spoon melted like candlewax
A woman kissing a badge
A child holding silence in both hands

None of that made sense
Then it all did.

In the dream, people stopped using names.
They pointed instead.
And if you said someone's name aloud,
the walls shivered.

I told my partner the next morning.
He laughed, kissed my forehead.
Called me oracle.

Two weeks later, he forgot my name.

Not like a joke.
Like it had never existed.

He called me "hey" and "you,"
and when I asked him what street we lived on,
he said,

"We live where the light is thin."

That's when I knew.

The dream was not a warning.
It was a receipt.

(Transcript ends. No follow-up recovered.)

She dreamed the end before it fell.
She saw the door. She knew the smell.

A vision stitched with fire and thread
Of things we burned before they bled.

Her warnings came in silence dressed.
The kind of truth we all suppressed.

If dreams are echoes cast ahead,
What do we owe the ones who said?

<u>Transcript Fragment 6 "The Child"</u>

(Voice Print: Unknown – Recorded during intake at Refuge Dusk, Age Estimated: 7)

The monster didn't have teeth.

It had a mouth, but it whispered your own voice back at you.

When I saw it, I wasn't scared.
I felt like I was late.

I tried to draw it for the lady,
but the crayon broke every time I got to the face.

She said I was just scared.
But I wasn't.

I saw Mommy walking into the dark,
and she said, "Don't forget the song."

But there was no song.
Just the hum.

I think the hum is what we forgot, not the words.

I don't know how to spell it,
but it's like the noise in your ear
when you're about to cry but don't.

The monster only came when people said "everything's fine."

I stopped saying that.

I started writing names on rocks.
I throw them into the quiet to keep it awake.

I think that's how you beat it.
You don't be brave.
You just remember out loud.

(Interview terminated. Guardian no longer present for consent. Transcript sealed.)

A child spoke of whispers shaped like breath,
Of hums that held the hands of death.

She never lied. She never guessed.
She named the silence, then she blessed.

I cannot draw the things she drew.
Her crayon cracked. My memory too.

If names are stones, and truth is play,
Then maybe that is how we stay.

Against the Quiet

We did not win.
There was no banner,
no broadcast,
no city reclaimed.

But we were the breathing left.

We walked.
We carried knives and names.
We slept with our backs against brick
and took turns pretending not to dream.

And when the wind moved wrong,
we moved anyway.

*I found a group that headed toward the north
with no trucks, no guns. Just set forth.*

*They didn't see me trailing from the side.
That's how you learn what people choose to hide.*

*I kept my distance, not too far to lose
the rhythm in the choices they would use.*

*I wrote what passed when no one watched them move
what stayed behind, what burdened, what they proved.*

*I never learned the names they didn't speak.
But how they walked told everything I seek.*

To Walk Is to Refuse

They step through doors that swing too slow,
our boots the only prayers we know.
A window breaks. No one looks back.
The sun is just another trap.

The road forgets it was a map.
A sign says "Help." It's just a scrap.
We learn to walk without a sound.
The wind has rules. We write them down.

One child ties knives into her sleeves.
One mother sleeps between the leaves.
We build a fire inside a mall.
We do not speak of what we saw.

And when we rest, we rest in pairs.
And when we sleep, we set our snares.
We do not name the days we pass
to walk is how we say: not yet.

I lost their shapes when dusk began to spill,
but followed the noise that stayed too still.

At every stop, I lingered where they slept
I listened close. I watched. I never wept.

I wrote down only what the moment gave
not fear, not hope, but what refused the grave.

These are the places scorched by memory's breath.
These are the steps that walked away from death.

We pass a house that sings with flies.
A doll still sits with bitten eyes.
We do not enter. Not for food.
The dead are loud. We've learned their mood.

The pumps are dry. The door's ajar.
We find a lighter in the yard.
The clerk is bones, his name tag gone.
We do not count how long he's worn.

The wind plays games along the bridge.
A coat is nailed to a concrete ridge.
We cross in twos. We do not look
at what still floats beneath the hook.

A chalkboard reads: Be kind. Be brave.
The desks are graves. The halls behave.
One girl salutes the empty class.
We take the globe. We let it pass.

We sleep beneath a plastic tree.
The food court ghosts know how to be.
A shoe store plays a looped refrain
buy one, get one. It sounds like pain.

The traffic light still blinks on red.
A sign says yield. We go instead.
The crosswalk beeps to no one's steps.
We trace the silence where it slept.

We reach the place where roads give out.
The grass is high. The trees don't doubt.
We do not ask what waits ahead.
We only walk. We are not dead.

I did not stay to see them sleep.
They'd earned the right to keep that deep.
I turned before the fire grew low
a shadow once, and once alone.

I followed them as far as I could stay.
They didn't see me leave. I slipped away.

That, too, is how the breathing learn to live
to take what's needed, give what they can give.

I found new prints. Smaller, slow, and unsure
with songs around their fires, soft and pure.

Their steps were different, but their oath the same:
to breathe is choice; to move is more than name.

I wrote the vows they whispered into air
the truths they taught instead of offered prayer.

this is what they swore

we swore to move.

even if the road cracked like a throat.
even if our names faded first.
even if there was no one left to say,
i remember.

we swore to breathe.

not just in lungs, but in hands.
in the way we warmed food.
in the way we kept watch.
in the way we still carried one spoon for joy.
we swore to bury only what could not follow.

we swore to walk.

we swore to walk until the silence changed shape.
until even the dead learned to step aside.

Inheritance

A coat too big.
A knife once dull.
A compass that spins but won't stop.
One story learned by heart.
Two footsteps always left behind.
Three wrong turns and still
we move.
Not to rebuild.
Just to outlive the stillness.

The blinds were closed, but something lit the glass.
A flicker, quiet, waiting for the pass.

I smelled canned beans and smoke and something sharp.
The kind of silence tuned a half-step dark.

I did not knock. I knew what waits for sound.
Some rooms survive by never being found.

Canto IV – The Quiet Fight

They did not shout. They did not raise a flag.
Their stories were not written down in stone.
They moved like breath across a sleeping crag.

No songs were sung. No names were widely known.
Their victories were small, were bread, were boots
were knives unthrown and fires lit alone.

One woman pulled her child through broken routes.
A boy laid wire where no map still applied.
A man fed three with crickets and with roots.

A girl repaired a bike her sister tried
to ride beyond the edge of what was marked.
A soldier woke to find his orders lied.

They moved through ash. They slept where metal sparked.
They shared one pair of shoes between them all.
Their stories were not straight. Their hope was dark.

One group lived weeks inside a shopping mall
a world of glass and mannequins and dust.
They left one prayer beneath an escalator stall.

A painter used their blood to mix the rust.
A singer hummed beneath a plastic dome.
A priest baptized survivors in the crust

of rain they caught in bowls of Styrofoam.
They spoke in signs. They rationed every sound.
Their shelter was a word, or sometimes "home."

One woman walked with nails inside her wound,
unstitched, unsealed, until she reached a fence.
They did not let her in. She turned around.

A boy drew maps in charcoal and in sense.
A girl lit candles shaped like ribs and bone.
A whisper passed for law, or consequence.

And I, who watched from ridge and shattered stone,
wrote only what survived the light of day
not heroics, but the way they walked alone.

One taught their friends to listen in delay
to wait a beat before they stepped or spoke.
Another learned to farm the mold and gray.

A mother wrote down rules she could revoke.
A child asked if zombies still could dream.
A guard betrayed the dead with just one stroke.

They fixed what still could break and not just seam.
They cooked with salt and silence and with shame.
They bartered bullets, cloth, and jars of cream.

They did not brag. They did not seek acclaim.
They took no selfies. None went live or bold.
They grieved in pairs. They made the ash their frame.

One kissed their wife beneath a bus turned cold.
One held their father's arm until it stilled.
One ran. One froze. One whispered what was told

to keep the youngest calm. One boy rebuilt
a water pump from parts he could not name.
One girl laid traps with berries and with guilt.

A knife was passed through hands that felt the same.
A rope was tied where hands had once held prayer.
A child said thank you but forgot their name.

They drew no flags. They built no new world fair.
They stitched old names into a coat, then left.
They vanished where the breathing thinned the air.

A woman climbed through sewers slick with theft
to bring a child aspirin and bread.
She smiled. She coughed. She never told the rest.

One carved their story on a closet's thread
not poems, not dates, just things they'd seen and kept.
A note said: Find the firewood near the shed.

Another taught herself the way she wept
not in sound, but through her hands in clay.
She shaped the faces of the ones who slept.

They walked in groups that did not often stay.
They passed through cities whittled down to bones.
They wrote directions no one dared obey.

A man played chess with rocks, ignored the moans.
He said, I win if I'm alive tomorrow.
He lost a rook, then started stacking stones.

They left behind instructions born from sorrow:
Boil twice. Don't trust the lights. The wind can lie.
And still they hoped, though not the kind you borrow.

They never said goodbye, just don't ask why.
They traded boots, and teeth, and threadbare luck.
They did not kneel, but learned the way to try.

A witness only, ghost among the stuck,
did not record their glory but their tread.
Their breath. Their pacing through what left them struck.

They are not gone. They are not wholly dead.
The world forgets; I remember each face
the breathing left, but something stronger led.

They etched new roads with footprints none would trace.
One child still played with pebbles in the dirt.
A woman counted ribs to mark her place.

Some planted seeds in boots once filled with hurt.
A boy found music in a crumpled can.
One tied a cloth where veins began to spurt.

They stitched new names into an old tin pan.
They boiled weeds twice, and once again for doubt.
They mapped the tunnels where no voice outran.

One man grew gardens in a bunker's drought.
Another raised a chick from out a shell.
They found a stream and bathed their silence out.

Some danced, then wept. Some kissed and would not tell.
A girl learned code with rusted wire and stones.
A mother folded paper just to spell

the names of those who walked with fractured bones.
A soldier built a bed from window glass.
A father taught his child to count the moans.

One held a match too long, and let it pass
to one who feared the dark but struck it still.
They learned the silence, like a kind of mass.

They stitched with thread and fishhooks and with will.
They walked past cities gutted into script.
One held a sign that simply said: "Be still."

A butcher carved in brick what the dying ripped
not elegy, not rage, but names they knew.
A sister dreamed her brother never slipped.

One woman tied old wires to her shoe
and sparked a bulb that blinked just once, then died.
A boy built traps with cardboard and with glue.

They did not say, "We lived." They only tried.
One girl gave birth in snow and did not scream.
A man read Psalms where paper had survived.

Some followed stars. Some followed only steam.
A cook made broth from pepper and from ash.
A boy escaped inside a salted dream.

They limped through dusk. They lit their fires in trash.
They shared what once was poisoned with the thin.
They told no tales that ended in a flash.

One woman stitched her heartbeat to her skin.
One drew a face on every can he tossed.
They saved no gold, no relics, only kin.

A girl with burns still counted what she'd lost.
A man forgave his mother in a note.
They carved directions deep into the frost.

They found old songs and hummed a single note.
One whistled through a pipe to mimic rain.
They wrapped the dead in coats and names and wrote.

They spoke of loss like one might speak of grain.
They learned the word for hunger, then for wait.
And still they stood, though crooked, though in pain.

I wrote their breath into the ash and thread.
Not songs, not triumphs, just the paths they tread.

They did not ask for monuments or flame.
They only kept the memory of names.

Some stitched their lives to tin, to cloth, to stone.
Some moved through fire just to die unknown.

But I remember. That's the vow I keep.
To write of those who walked instead of weep.

They fought, but not in ways the world would show.
They fought in silence. In the dirt. Below.

One whispered, write me like the wind I crossed.
I did. And still I mourn the breath they lost.

So when you read this, do not bow or cry.
Just breathe once more. Then let that be reply.

Their fight was quiet. Still, it filled the sky.
And I'm the last to write it, not the why.

Some losses weren't a war, but just a room.
A fire flickered. Then it made more gloom.

Not every end came with a scream or flight.
Some came with forks. With lullabies. With night.

A girl once wrote a story on her skin.
A boy drew faces just to trap things in.

One family stayed too long beside the trees.
They hoped the locks would teach the dead to freeze.

I do not know what made them stay, or pray.
I only know the flame was not enough that day.

What follows next is not for proof or song.
Just memory that said, they didn't last that long.

The Last Lamplight

The dusk had bled into the trembling pines,
As wind howled dirges through the window seam,
And something scratched the camper's metal spines.

The lantern hissed, a fragile, flickering dream
That cast long shadows on the cupboard door,
Where father nailed a cross and mouthed a scream.

The children wept upon the vinyl floor,
Their mother clutching salt like sacred ash,
While silence pooled outside like something more.

Then tapping came; not knuckles, more a lash
A slither-press of hands with broken bone,
Soft laughter bleeding through a static flash.

"We're not alone," she whispered in a tone
That glass might use before it shatters cold,
And dad just aimed his shotgun at the drone.

The boy, too young to speak, grew strangely bold
He drew a stick man on the fogged-up pane,
Its eyes twin voids too old for him to hold.

The knocks became a symphony of pain,
Each beat a nail torn from the walls outside,
Till campers creaked beneath the crimson rain.

The mother prayed; the father stood with pride;
The door blew wide, the lantern's flame went black,
And from the dark, the dead began to slide.

They fought with forks and books and panicked smack,
But shadows swarmed like wolves who'd smelt despair
Each breath was razored, each retreat cut back.

The father roared and fired into the air.
The girl screamed, "Go!" but there was no escape.
The boy just stared at something none could bear.

Then silence. Just the cold night taking shape,
The camper shushed beneath the trembling trees.
Its roof half gone. Its world now draped in gape.

And on the glass, beneath the mold and freeze,
The stick man smiled, its arms stretched wide with glee,
As if to say, "They never stood a breeze."

Anatomy of the Dead III

The hands curl inward
when they die.
We call it reverence,
though it's only bone remembering its grip.

Some hands still reach for bowls.
Some for throats.
Some try to braid the hair they miss.

Under the fingernails
soil,
blood,
a thread of someone else's sweater.

They don't know what they held.
But they keep trying to offer it back.

There is no tremble.
No reverence.
Only the motion of having once mattered.

We Move

We move because we still are not the dead.
The sky forgets its name. The ground forgets.
We carry hunger like a kind of thread.

The maps are ash. The rivers burn instead.
A child repeats the names her mother lets.
We move because we still are not the dead.

Our mouths are dry. Our footsteps shout ahead.
The trees watch silently as light resets.
We carry hunger like a kind of thread.

No gods remain. No orders to be read.
We find a rusted can and make our bets.
We move because we still are not the dead.

We mark the roads in chalk and borrowed lead.
Our stories float where certainty forgets.
We carry hunger like a kind of thread.

Don't call it life. Don't name it hope or dread.
We walk. That's all. The breathing not regrets.
We move because we still are not the dead.
We carry hunger like a kind of thread.

                              Keep

                on

           walking

Companions Lost

A girl named nothing walked barefoot through the grime.
Her hair was leaves, her clothes were stitched from mist.
She spoke in signs and sang in crooked rhyme.

We shared one fire beneath the old assist
of gasless lights and fallen metal towers.
She said, "You live if you can still exist."

She shaped small animals with threads and flowers.
She gave me one and said its name was stay.
She vanished by the edge of dawn's cold hours.

A boy called Flint could mimic light and clay.
He carved illusions in the fog with sticks.
He danced where silence tried to steal away.

He claimed he'd kissed a ghost and felt the fix
of memory return like wine to gut.
He read my poems and laughed in nervous ticks.

I found a man who slept inside a hut
he made from doors of vans and layered bone.
He hummed to jars of rain and never shut.

He spoke in math. His numbers held their own
like psalms. He etched equations on the rock.
He taught me how to solve for left alone.

A woman named Marielle walked like chalk.
Her step was soft, her hands both firm and bruised.
She told old jokes, then paused before the knock.

She kept her journal sealed and rarely used
but once she read aloud a line on grief:
It lingers not to hurt, but stay confused.

I met a pair who called their team Belief.
They held a mirror broken into three.
They said, "We're made of wrong, but not of thief."

They burned their past each week beneath a tree.
They whispered names, then watched them leave like birds.
They hugged me once, then passed without decree.

A child named Penn had never learned of words.
He drew in circles, stacked his thoughts in stone.
He gave me one. It pulsed like soft unheard.

One boy and girl lived high in towers grown
from vines they braided tight as braided love.
They taught each bee to buzz a certain tone.

They shared with me their symphony of dove
a music stitched from wind and wood and sting.
They said, "You'll find the heart in what it shoves."

One man I met had lost his need to cling.
He walked in silence, shared a piece of bark.
He wrote one word, then gave the word a wing.

The word was with. He smiled, then left the dark.
I copied it inside my shoulder blade.
I carried it through alleyways and lark.

Some lasted hours. Some remained and stayed.
Some taught me how to gather rain in cups.
Some left me songs to play when echoes fade.

One gave me seeds and said, "Ignore the ups."
He meant the hills, the guards, the drones, the wrath.
He said, "Just plant them anywhere, and trust."

And I, the poet, chronicled each path
not just the loss, but where the hands had met.
Their breath, their fire, their jokes that made me laugh.

Each name I knew I etched without regret.
Not saints. Not heroes. Just the ones who tried.
Their kindness lit the corners they beget.

*I thought I'd seen all forms that life could take.
I hadn't. This was new. And built to hide fake.*

*They called it Safe. Each letter carved with care
the kind of word you'd paste on folding chairs.*

*Walls. White tents. And grins too wide.
Their food had dates, but none they verified.*

*A man with forms asked if I had a cough.
I asked if songs still stirred their voices soft.*

*He didn't laugh. He checked another box.
His hands were clean. His questions came in flocks.*

*They let me through. My bag was weighed, then tagged.
A woman marked my name but didn't ask.*

*I didn't write. Not yet. The air was thin
too many eyes, too many teeth in grin.*

*But I observed the way they washed their hands,
the way the gates made every footstep planned.*

*The children played, but never left the tape.
Their laughter came in shapes that don't escape.*

Their joy was quiet, boxed and soft and small.
Their stories ended neatly, if at all.

A man recited rules beside the flame.
He wore no badge, but everyone knew his name.

He said: Survival is a shape we choose.
I wrote: Control is just another bruise.

They lit their fires like rehearsed applause.
They bowed to order, never asked its cause.

I saw no weapons. Just a stack of forms.
Just sterilized routine to mimic storms.

I know this much: Stillness is just a pose.
And something in the silence always knows.

Sanctioned Breaths

The doors sealed soft,
like good manners.

They smiled as they locked us in.

We were clean, contained,
approved by the breathing machines.
No one asked why the air tasted like bleach.
No one asked about the missing.

We Were Grateful to Be Safe

I. Smile when spoken to.
II. Avoid prolonged eye contact.
III. Do not open the doors
IV. Repeat the phrase: "We're grateful to be safe."
V. Do not say "freedom."
VI. Do not say "before."
VII. Stay where the cameras can see you.

Canto V – Silence behind the Fence

They called it safe, and hung the sign in gold.
The tents were white. The ground was freshly swept.
Each welcome came rehearsed, and never bold.

A child smiled wide, but never truly wept.
The food was wrapped with numbers, clean and clear.
The rules were posted. Everyone had slept.

A clipboard clicked whenever one drew near.
A cough was met with silence and a glance.
The loud were labeled risk. The soft were dear.

The leader spoke of hope and second chance,
his teeth too white, his voice too tightly strung.
He praised the fence and order and advance.

A woman served each meal with practiced tongue.
Her apron bore a name she did not choose.
Her hands were slow. Her wedding ring had swung

beside her tray, untouched, too clean to use.
The soldiers lined the pathways with their eyes.
Their guns were oiled. Their boots looked almost new.

One boy was lost for asking what was left unseen.
He drew the word outside in dusty script.
By morning it was gone, and so was he.

They spoke in hymns that did not quite equip
the truth: that doors could lock from either side.
Their kindness came in forms of calm and grip.

I watched a man get punished for his pride
not loudly, not with force, but lack of place.
They simply let the warnings coincide

with isolation, smiles, and measured grace.
He vanished on patrol. No one was blamed.
The files showed a blank, a time, a space.

A girl in red asked softly why we named
this place a Zone instead of calling it
a town, or home, or something less inflamed.

No one replied. She disappeared a bit
each day her shoes, her voice, her way to laugh.
Her stories dulled. Her light began to split.

The schoolhouse bore a mural cut in half.
A sun. A face. A child with upraised hand.
The rest was scrubbed to gray and folded back.

The radio still played its pre-planned band.
Announcements, hymns, a voice that spoke of care.
It told us where to walk, to sit, to stand.

And I the one who stayed but did not stare
who whispered poems into folding air
I wrote the peace that sounded like despair.

The beds were made. The linens smelled like soap.
A mother rocked, though no one knew her child.
We fed the plants with rationed bits of hope.

A man once screamed. They said he had gone wild.
They gave his name to someone newly born.
The form was filed. The bulletin was mild.

The children drew the fence with loops and thorns.
They colored guards as giants without eyes.
The sun was always orange, the sky was worn.

One woman kept a journal of the lies.
She pressed dried leaves inside to mark the days.
It vanished when she questioned "how" and "why."

The guards wore smiles that didn't quite appraise
but followed backs too long, too close, too still.
One blink could mark your file in subtle ways.

We cheered on cue. We rationed every thrill.
We praised the silence more than sound or song.
We learned to call compliance human will.

And I, who counted dusk as something wrong,
remained to feel the quiet turning strong.

They called it peace. I knew it by its weight.
Not loud, but always watching, always late.

The quiet here was cleaner than the ash.
It held no screams, just glances sharp as glass.

They smiled too often. No one sang off-key.
The children drew in gray. No one asked me.

The rules were rules, and not just for the dead.
We praised the walls, then stared at them instead.

One man once said, "At least it's not out there."
I nodded, but the silence wasn't fair.

I wrote in corners no one thought to sweep.
I kept the names they filed away too deep.

And when the loudspeaker began to hum,
I knew which voice was next. I did not come.

Order

        Within these walls, the wind forgets to bite.
        The soil grows calm beneath a painted fence.
        We serve the morning wrapped in perfect light
        our voices low, our boundaries immense.

The gates are strong. Our rosters hold their names.
    We speak of duty more than pain or loss.
    We mourn in measured hours, not in flames.
    Our gardens bloom without the threat of cost.

We've scrubbed the maps of ruin, ash, and waste.
    Our children do not dream of teeth or fire.
    We walk in lines. We teach them order's taste.
    They do not run. They do not look for higher.

And though the world still burns beyond our view,
    the fire knows now it does not pass through you.

Such a moving speech, so smooth, so grand
he almost made me clap with my one free hand.

To be unseen is better than control
I slip between the cracks they say are whole.

I heard his "Order." Every line precise,
but there were teeth behind that polished ice.

The way he breathed between his perfect sounds,
the pause that begged for something not around

I wrote it down. The words he chose to say.
But what he didn't, that's what gave him away.

I'll mark which words he writes but never speaks,
the moments when his faith begins to leak.

I'll linger where the cameras never turn,
and trace the shadows masked behind concern.

Let others praise the fences, gates, and law.
I'll take my notes; name the cracks I saw.

So I will watch him when he thinks alone
the way his fingers twitch around the throne.

The Silence Beyond the Fence

They nod when I appear.
They do not blink.
Their stillness is a kind of gratitude.

It frightens me.

I never meant to build a place
where no one speaks unless allowed.

The gate still creaks.
We oil it every day,
as if the sound itself would let them in

them

the ones who move without remembering
how breath should work,
how hunger should behave.

I've learned to speak in metrics,
not in words.

They like instructions more than memory.
Emotion makes them shift.

I see it now

the flicker in the eyes,
the lowered hands,

the way they hold their children
like they're bags of food,
not stories waiting to unfold.

A boy today refused to kneel for song.

He said the wind outside
was cleaner than the one
we bottle here in paper masks.

I smiled.
I took his name.
I marked the list.

There's nothing wrong.
We live.
The power holds.
But I have started waking when it's dark.
Not from a scream, not from any noise.
From nothing.
That's the thing I fear the most.

I saw him standing, talking to the wall
the part where names are listed when they fall.

He fixed his coat. He straightened every seam.
He told the dark, "It's working." A dream.

I think he knows the silence isn't right.
I think he's asking mirrors how to fight.

His garden's neat. His hands are always clean.
But what he buries never stays unseen.

And when he speaks again to name what's whole
you'll hear the cracking through the role.

The Places Safety Leaks

The birds returned, but none remembered song.
They peck at glass, like they forget the sky.
We say, "it's fine," and smile a little wrong.
The children count their steps, but never why.

A man removed his mask too close to dusk.
A woman laughed too loudly near the gate.
We fed them warnings, silence, then the husk
of protocol dressed up as measured fate.

The ground still hums. The pipes still choke at night.
A child drew teeth beneath the school's new crest.
A guard looked up and wept beneath the light.
We called it fog. He hasn't since confessed.

He makes his speech. Shapes it clean and wide.
He does not name the ones who live outside.

In the Dust of Safety

They built a zone with banners made of code.
The gates were white. The fences sang in light.
They named each path and sterilized the road.

The signs said "Welcome," bordered clean and bright.
Each tent the same. Each window sealed with grace.
The grass was cut to a uniform height.

They said, "You're safe," and never showed their face.
They scanned our eyes for things they wouldn't name.
They taught us how to breathe in measured pace.

A mother asked if grief could be a flame.
They gave her pills and told her not to think.
Her child was listed wrong. She took the blame.

We lined up twice for water, thrice for ink.
Each week we knelt for "Thought Correction Hour."
The loud were sent to rooms without a link.

A woman spoke of freedom as a flower.
The guards took notes. She left with stitched up lips.
They said her metaphor abused her power.

Each corner bore a screen with prayerful clips
recycled joy, approved from archive vaults.
One showed a man who danced, then fainted mid-skip.

His file said: Defective Moral Faults.
We heard the noise when doors would seal too tight.
We learned to smile through sanitized assaults.

I knew a boy who questioned day and night.
He asked why songs all ended the same.
They found his cot unzipped and lost from sight.

The food was tagged with numbers, not a name.
The apples gleamed, but none had taste or bruise
The soup was gray. The hunger stayed the same.

A woman served with hands too slow, abused
by years of trays and silence and her ring.
She wore her nameplate backward. We excused.

The leader wore a pin shaped like a wing.
He spoke of hope, of fences, of a plan.
His words stitched with nothing to which you could cling.

He praised the order born from final scan.
He said, "Our chaos died so we could thrive."
He said this while they dragged away a man.

They told us not to question those who drive.
They gave us scripts for grieving, praise, and sleep.
They banned all stories written to survive.

We met at night in corners cold and deep.
We whispered lines in fragments, half-remembered.
We fed on tales forbidden we could keep.

A girl in red grew slowly dismembered
not in body, but in what she was.
Her laughter dulled. Her name grew disencumbered.

Each day she lost a piece, a nail, a clause.
Her voice turned thin. Her gaze became a wall.
She asked, "Why Zones and not a town, because?"

But no one spoke. Her question was her fall.
She vanished from the mess hall and the list.
Her blanket folded soft and small. That's all.

And I, the poet, lived on just to twist
my lines in places guards would never see.
My rhymes were warnings dressed as quiet mist.

I wrote with water on a rationed knee.
I scratched out couplets in a paper roll.
Each verse disguised as prayers for decree.

They never caught me, but they took a toll.
I lost three teeth to hunger and to ink.
My bones forgot the way they used to stroll.

Yet still I write though pressed against the brink
to mark that safety can be just a cage,
a place to keep your soul from how you think.

I found this tucked beneath a tray of masks
the kind they give, but never dare to ask.

Burned at the edge, its ink half-eaten through,
but grief survives in every blocked-out clue.

They crossed out names. They blacked out breath and blame.
But what remained still carried heat and name.

They thought the dark could make the past behave.
But paper hums the things we failed to save.

REDACTED: Sector Report #03–9E

▮▮▮ no breach at checkpoint ▮▮▮
▮▮▮▮▮▮▮▮▮▮▮▮▮▮▮▮▮▮▮▮▮▮
▮▮▮ she looked familiar ▮▮▮
▮▮▮ we didn't ▮▮▮ spread ▮▮▮ fast ▮▮▮
▮▮▮ doors sealed ▮▮▮
▮▮▮ protocol ▮▮▮
▮▮▮ screaming persisted ▮▮ then stopped ▮▮▮
▮▮▮ believed ▮▮▮
▮▮▮ not really ▮▮▮
▮ we couldn't ▮▮▮ him ▮▮
▮▮▮ the guard ▮▮ the fire ▮▮▮
▮▮▮ We told them ▮▮ containable ▮▮▮
▮▮▮ we lied ▮▮▮ lied ▮▮▮
▮▮▮ we lied ▮▮▮

The White That Covered What We Wouldn't Say

The white that covered what we wouldn't say
was quiet, bright, and far too close to clean.
The rules were sharp. The walls would never fray.

They taught us how to kneel, then look away.
They fed us sleep and called the silence green.
The white that covered what we wouldn't say

was stitched across the mouth of yesterday.
The gates were locked. The air was sipped between.
The rules were sharp. The walls would never fray.

A man was taken just for turning gray.
A woman's cough was scrubbed from every screen.
The white that covered what we wouldn't say

dripped down like mercy wrapped in soft decay.
They called it peace. We knew it was routine.
The rules were sharp. The walls would never fray.

They smiled while painting over those who'd stray.
We prayed in gowns, our hands already clean.
The white that covered what we wouldn't say
the rules were sharp. The walls would never fray.

Betrayal & Fire

It wasn't the match.
It was the hand that struck it
and the smile
that watched it burn.
We used to believe
betrayal had a sound.
But it was quiet
like a house turning to ember
with the door left
open.

They Came Through the Mirrors

They don't knock. They reflect.

I look in the mirror
and see my brother ixing his hair.
He's humming something from before
something soft,
something wrong.

In one dream, I clean the glass
and find my father brushing his teeth.
But the toothpaste is black.

My sister smiles
from the bathroom sink.
She keeps brushing the same tooth.
Over and over.
It's not hers.

The mirrors don't crack. They ripple.

Someone calls my name
but it sounds like a drawer being pulled too far.

In the last dream, I turn away.
I face the wall.
I hear the mirror breathing behind me.

And still, I wake up
with fog on the glass.

Recognition

The child called a name.

The body turned.

Maybe it smiled.
Maybe it didn't.

The door clicked.

The guards were gone.
Flame needs no plan.

Only an opening.

Only love.

Someone Opened the Door

I heard the click.

Not a scream. Not glass.
Just the sound of choosing.

Someone opened the door.
The hallway remembered
what fear sounded like.

It started with a voice.
Soft. High.

"That's her," the child said.
"That's my friend."

No one stopped him.
We didn't know we needed to.

She was standing just beyond the line.
Wearing a bow.
And her mouth.
And her name.

He turned the latch like it was a gift.
The door gasped.
And so did we.

The dead came in
without rage.

Just heat.

The fire started where the kitchens kept sugar.

Someone struck the match,
but who was watching then?

We didn't cry.
We blamed.
We burned.

I saw the boy again, later.
In the courtyard.

Holding her hand.
Or what was left of it.

It wasn't treason. Not a coup, nor scheme.
No plot concealed beneath a rebel's dream.

No wires cut. No passwords passed along.
Just silence, and a memory held too strong.

A boy who knew a girl who used to sing.
He saw her bow. He missed the broken thing.

No hunger drove it. Not revenge or flame.
Just one small voice still calling out her name.

And one hand reached, because it thought it should.
Because once, reaching meant something good.

inhale

the

silence

Canto VI – The Door That Knew His Name

It wasn't rage that brought the fire in.
It wasn't war. It wasn't teeth or plot.
The gate stayed closed, but love undid the pin.

A child stood where every guard forgot.
He saw a face beneath the burning sun
too torn to be named, too quiet to be not.

He knew that face. Or thought he did. The run
they used to do in alleys past the school.
A ribbon. Shoes. A single hand, undone.

The guards were far. The kitchen smelled of fuel.
A pot had tipped. A spark beneath the tray.
The leader prayed. The radios kept cool.

The child called out: You're late again. It's play.
He didn't flinch. He did not feel the ash.
The gate swung wide. The dead did not delay.

They walked on fire. Their eyes were split with flash.
Their skin was flaking, bright with silent heat.
One dropped a jaw. Another dragged a sash

once worn to prom, now fused into her meat.
They did not speak, but moved with deadly grace
no hunger now, no hurry in their feet.

The fence gave way like paper cut from place.
The alarms began to blink, not scream.
A mother closed her window, just in case.

The guards returned too late to catch the seam
where air turned fire, and memory turned lie.
The doctor dropped his chart and broke his beam.

The child stood still. He didn't even cry.
A woman tried to pull him back, but not in time.
His voice was last to echo, not to die.

A scream began, but didn't end in rhyme.
The radios began to loop a hymn.
The leader whispered, This was not the crime.

The streets caught flame. The tents grew faint and dim.
The pantry doors collapsed. The signs unpinned.
The sky went black. The skyline blurred its brim.

A soldier aimed, but wouldn't shoot his friend.
A medic ran with sheets and open arms.
A child was locked inside to meet the end.

One father begged, Don't shoot. She means no harm.
A window cracked. The pressure changed the room.
A hallway caught like kindling, warm with charm.

The gates gave in. The tower met its doom.
The speaker stammered, then just played a tone.
A girl was found still singing through the gloom.

The kitchen, first to light, was last to moan.
A recipe was written on the wall.
The onions blackened near the father's phone.

The fire spread in loops, in waves, in crawl.
It danced with ash, it dressed in breathless heat.
It burned the beds. It touched the prayerful hall.

And I watched from where the hilltop meets
the memory of fences, gates, and name.
I saw what love invites when safety cheats.

It wasn't rage that brought the dead to flame.
A single word that called a ghost by name.

Her Ribbon Was the Same

I didn't know.

She looked like before.
The same shoes.
The same braid.

She waved at me.
She remembered.

No one else did.

They all looked through me
like glass.
But she smiled.
Even if her teeth were wrong.

I wanted her inside.
That's what friends do.

I didn't know.
I didn't know
I didn't

<u>Anatomy of the Dead IV</u>

The feet blister.
Then heal without knowing why.

They walk.
Always toward something
they used to wait for.

We have followed tracks
that lead nowhere
except to doorsteps,
backyards,
swings.

One girl's shoes
were worn thin on one side only.
She limped, but in rhythm
the rhythm of school bells,
of skipping songs,
of waiting in line.

The feet forget their names
but not the routes.
They turn left at the smell of chalk.
They hesitate at the edge of hopscotch squares.

They pause at every place
where joy once left them.

Some doors were shut to hold the world at bay.
This one was closed to keep a friend away.

He knew her name. He let the silence in.
And still I'd choose his kindness over other sin.

The dead will come through anger just as fast
but his was love, and I will let that last.

They Let Them In

They didn't just

unlock the gate.

And when the dead came

through the smoke,

They circled time.

They called it

fate.

I saw him freeze, one hand upon the frame,
his lips unsure of whether breath or name.

He looked inside and knew what he would be:
not savior, not survivor. Just the key.

His face became the silence of the room,
the kind that knows it's choosing who meets doom.

There Was No Right Answer

It's still me.

I said your name

You reached for the handle.

I thought you were saving me.

I heard the clicks.

It smelled like smoke and something sweet.

I waited for you to open it again.

I pressed my hand to the glass.

You were still there.

Was I wrong? Was I bad?

It was just a door.
It was just my friend.

I kept walking. I did not write his name.
Some grief is smoke. And some becomes a flame.

They speak of "safe" as though it still exists
behind clean walls, in homes that don't resist.

But I have seen what "safe" begins to cost:
a child behind a door, a city lost.

I've watched their checkpoints drawn in perfect chalk
then watched the wind erase them as I walk.

They build new fences, raise their voices high,
as if commands could quiet how we die.

No place is safe. Not when the dead are near.
Not when our choices break beneath our fear.

He Knew Her Name

He knew her name and thought she knew his too.
Her ribbon was the same. Her smile was wrong.
We didn't stop him. What were we to do?

The gate was just a line he walked straight through.
The dead don't rush. They simply wait too long.
He knew her name and thought she knew his too.

A fire doesn't ask if you approve.
It only asks which memory feels strong.
We didn't stop him. What were we to do?

She stood there humming something old and blue.
Her mouth was not where it belonged.
He knew her name and thought she knew his too.

He waved. She waved. The sky forgot its hue.
A child's love can make the dead belong.
We didn't stop him. What were we to do?

I watched the guard decide, then follow through.
Regret is just another kind of song.
He knew her name and thought she knew his too.
We didn't stop him. What were we to do?

It started in the kitchen, near the door
a flicker that the oven didn't store.

A towel caught. No panic. Just a curse.
A leader muttered, "Could have been worse."

But flames don't wait for orders, don't report.
They leap like truth. too fast to cut or sort.

I watched it thread the hall like whispered doubt,
then kiss a vent and carry itself out.

The roof inhaled. The windows turned to breath.
One building flared a signal dressed as death.

Then smoke began to wander, not to rise,
and smoke curled upward, softening the skies.

A siren hiccupped. Radios went blind.
Some ran. Some stayed. Some resigned.

And just like that, the plan they built from fear
ignited at the edge, soon to disappear.

The Fire Didn't Stop Them

I saw it from the ridge
the Safe Zone, lit like promise,
turning orange with consequence.

The flames began in kitchens,
where sugar and memory live.

I watched the roofs dissolve
into ash-light,
watched shadows rise behind the walls
like puppets uncut from their strings.

Someone screamed "They're burning!"

But the dead don't choke.

They walked out through the fire
still lit,
eyes black and boiling,
skin crackling like old maps.

They carried flame in their bones
and spread it like religion.

Every house opened.
Every siren failed.

A child tried to crawl beneath a car
and found her father already there
lit from within,
reaching.

The guard tower fell.
The fence melted into teeth.

No orders now. No gates to close.
Only hunger wearing fire like skin.

And in the end,

what they built to keep the dead away
only fed the blaze
that brought them closer.

<u>Ashen Rite</u>

The gate was left ajar, but no one screamed.
A child had smiled and whispered, "She has come."
The sky went white, as if the world had dreamed.

A siren sang, too late, too slow, too numb.
The air turned sweet, like meat left out too long.
The guards were gone, their rifles picked up some.

And then she walked a girl, or maybe wrong,
her shoes too small, her breath a furnace spark.
The crowd just stared. Her mouth was not a song.

She moved like lullabies dissected dark,
each step a cleaver, soft with satin's pace.
Her bow was red. Her eyes were burned to mark.

A man knelt down. "You lost?" She showed her face.
It peeled, not wholly wrong, but far from right.
He never stood again. Just fell, in place.

They came behind her limping in the light
that turned to flame the longer you would look.
One woman wept, then vanished from the sight.

The preacher screamed and threw his holy book.
It turned to ash before it touched the ground.
A child laughed and dropped a garden hook.

Inside the school, the clock refused to sound.
The hands had stopped, or learned the art of dread.
The bells were full of soot and voiceless pound.

One nurse still wrote her charts. She wrote, "All dead."
She wrote it twice, then smeared the words with tea.
She held a match but lit her throat instead.

They gathered at the gates but did not flee.
The doors had learned to open only in.
And what came through was rot's theology.

A dog stood firm but lacked the will to sin.
He howled, then lay beneath a melted slide.
The ash fell down like prayers without skin.

A father kissed his wife and ran outside.
She followed but the flame had closed the gap.
Their names still echo where the porch rails dried.

The broadcast voice began to scream through sap,
the wires melting from their brittle posts.
"Remain indoors." Then static's final snap.

The chapel bells rang once for ghosts, for hosts.
The pews collapsed beneath a swarming song.
One boy said, "I can see my brother's ghosts."

The mirrors cracked, but never broke too long.
They showed the room, but never showed your face.
A teacher ran, but ran into the wrong.

A man crawled through the grass and begged for grace.
His body bloomed with bite-marks like a crown.
He said, "They eat your voice, then leave no trace."

A little girl still wore her party gown.
She danced where bodies fused into the wall.
She giggled, sang, then turned the system down.

The firefight began near City Hall.
The shots went wide, then stopped. The ash was thick.
A hand still clutched a spoon inside the sprawl.

They found a mother counting, "One, two, pick."
Her teeth were strange Her eyes were red.
She kissed her child and chose which one to stick.

The marketplace went silent. All had fled.
The fruit carts burned. The coins began to scream.
And sugar melted holes into the bread.

The baker sang a hymn of flour and steam.
Then bit the flour bag and sucked it dry.
His apron bore the name: Delicious Dream.

The sky turned green. The pigeons could not fly.
They walked in circles, speaking only mine.
One dropped a beak before it learned to cry.

They saw a man who'd swallowed wire line.
It coiled inside his gut like sacred thread.
He smiled and said, "I've tied it to the spine."

A girl was trapped beneath a crate marked Bread.
She said, "Don't help. I'm learning how to live."
She breathed out poems only she had read.

The guards lit flares, but none knew how to give
a plan that didn't start with burn or lie.
They said, "Comply. Obey. Receive. Forgive."

And then the dead began to organize.
Their hands unbroken by the rules of rest.
Their march composed of teeth and orphaned cries.

A wall collapsed. The census lost its guest.
The last record read: "Status incomplete."
A wristband buzzed. A voice said, "Please request"

But nothing more. The desk had caught the heat.
A smile was printed on a badge for health.
It melted with the flesh beneath the seat.

One man screamed, "Take my organs. Take my wealth!"
Then fed himself into the housing chute.
A scream came out. His jaw came next, by stealth.

The child who'd opened all of this stood mute.
His friend was gone, or never had been real.
He stared at flames and clutched a broken flute.

The general declared: "We do not kneel."
Then kneeled. Then screamed. Then whispered out a name.
Then kissed the floor as if it might reveal.

The anthem played, but never reached the same.
Its chorus dropped, replaced by shrieks and drone.
Each syllable became a scream of blame.

The doctor's chart was carved in brittle bone.
It read, "We lost the protocol to hope."
Each patient burned beneath a plastic cone.

The fire climbed the archive's wooden slope.
It sang in sparks. It sang in cursive flame.
A name was saved. The rest? No microscope.

And when the ashes cooled, they found one name
engraved beneath the fountain's marble lie:
"This wasn't hell. It simply played the same."

The square was silent. No one left to try.
Just statues dressed in soot and ruined thread.
The pigeons circled, asking, "Why not die?"

A child's handprint blackened one shed.
It dripped. It pulsed. It wouldn't dry or fade.
The sign beside it read: Evac instead.

And somewhere, far beyond the fire brigade,
a dog emerged dragging in jaw its tongue.
It dropped it at a gate. The gate obeyed.

The traitor's name was never sung or sung.
He lit the match and never said the word.
And in his heart, the child was always young.

The zone still stands, or stands beneath the blurred.
And those who come may ask what made it fall.
But all that's left is ash, and what's inferred.

I did not run. I did not call below.
The fire taught me more than fear could show.

I watched the walls collapse into the flame.
I did not shout. I did not take the blame.

Some things must fall. Some places must be lost.
The gates we build all carry silent cost.

I turned and walked. The dead don't chase the still.
The living do and that's what breaks the will.

Safe Zone, Remains

I do not name the dead, only the doorways they left ajar,
thresholds where hope once whispered and now wind passes through.

I do not write the names of streets; they folded into themselves,
curled like leaves in flame, their letters reduced to drifting soot.

I do not carry the rules they clung to like gospel,
for even scripture warps in heat, and silence made its own commandments.

I do not bury the ones who burned; I could not find the bodies.
They stood. They walked. They vanished with the fire still inside them.

I stayed behind when the others ran,
watching as the flames turned memory into smoke that does not rise.

I saw a child cradling a spoon softened by heat,
as if it were a relic of the world that still fed us.

I saw a man kneel before a wall like it might grant absolution,
though all it offered was ash, and the quiet echo of his breath.

I saw a woman kiss her badge as if it were lips,
then walk calmly into fire, her name never shouted.

I could have screamed. I almost did.
Instead, I turned to ink. I turned to paper. I turned away.

What they built was not a lie. It simply could not last.
Belief is not a barrier. Hope is not flameproof.

And I, the last to leave, write this without witness,
not to honor, not to condemn,
but to leave behind one soft thread for the wind to forget more slowly.

No names remain. No bells. No final sound.
Just silence kneeling where the flames were found.

Let silence fold its hands and bow its head.

The Ones Who Chose Not To

They did not wait for the gate to fall.
They did not test the bite,
or count the hours.

They saw the wind shift,
and laid down before the silence could take them.

Some wrote notes.
Some folded blankets.
Some just walked into the hush.

We do not know if it was weakness.
We only know
they were not among the screaming.

Memory

Memory is a fragile thread,
a lantern's fading light;
it lingers where the lost have fled,
and guards the coming night.

It holds the broken tales,
the whispers never told;
a map of distant trails,
in embers dim and cold.

Though silence tries to bind,
the past will not let go;
in memory we find
the seeds to help us grow.

The Woman at the Window

She watched the smoke curl
against the bruised sky,
a slow ribbon dissolving
into the evening's sigh.

The kettle whispered,
soft steam rising like breath
from a body learning to still.

Her hands moved carefully
a cup, a saucer,
the page of a notebook she opened
but did not finish.

No goodbyes were written.
Only lines,
half-formed shapes
that lingered between thought and silence.

Outside, the wind shifted,
carrying the distant moans
she had long stopped naming.

Her eyes traced
the shape of shadows
that slipped along the walls,
soft and slow,
as if time itself
had grown too tired to hurry.

She folded her fingers,
not in prayer,
but as if holding something fragile
a memory, a hope, a fading song
that might outlast the dark.

The chair cradled her like a quiet question,
and the room folded around her
like the last light before dark.

The clock ticked,
its sound a faint pulse
beneath the hush of evening.

Time slipped through the window,
slow and unhurried,
and for a moment,
everything simply was.

Between the cries and silent tears,
we hold the space of vanished years.

Not all who falter make a sound,
some choose the quiet underground.

A whispered breath, a fading star,
the end is near, yet hearts wander far.

In shadowed rooms where silence grows,
the weight of a loss no one knows.

No need for thunder, screams, or light
some battles end in softer night.

The Choir Who Kept Singing

They sang beneath the sky's unraveling thread,
in robes of soot and harmonies grown thin.
The pews were cracked. The hymnbooks had been read.

No congregation left to raise the dead,
no candlelight to drown the dark within.
They sang beneath the sky's unraveling thread.

Each voice a match that dared the hush to spread,
a chord struck clean where sermons had worn thin.
The pews were cracked. The hymnbooks had been read.

Their notes rang out like names no one had said,
a kind of prayer for what could not begin.
They sang beneath the sky's unraveling thread.

No one came to hush them or to dread
their final chorus lifting past the din.
The pews were cracked. The hymnbooks had been read.

And when the silence came, it bowed its head.
They sang, then vanished, mouths still shaped to sing.
They sang beneath the sky's unraveling thread.
The pews were cracked. The hymnbooks had been read.

The One Who Folded Maps

She believed the world could be folded
like linen,
or lungs,
or an apology left too long
in the throat.
Her hands always smelled
like old ink.

Borders creased.
Rivers rerouted with a sigh.
She made mountains vanish
by pressing them gently
between two thumbs.

Her room became a geography
of absence.

Shelves of silence.
A globe with its axis snapped.
No windows.

Only coordinates
that did not exist
until she named them.

In the end,
she folded
herself
inward.

We found a single note,
flat as breath:

"Everywhere was always too wide."

She tried to fold the world into a sigh,
to draw a border no one walked nearby.

Her fingers bent what names could not defend,
until her maps began to write the end.

I traced the creases, soft with use and dust,
and found no home. Just hope reduced to ust.

The Man Who Unplugged Everything

He pulled each socket
like weeds from a poisoned field.
Silence was his seed.

No bulbs. No beeps. No hum.
He fed candles to the dark.
The dark did not speak.

Fridge, radio, phone
he buried their quiet bones
beneath floorboards deep.

Neighbors begged for news.
He said, "Signals are baited traps."
Then cut his own door.

Each day: one less hum.
Each night: his heartbeat louder.
He learned not to flinch.

The final unplug
his own voice. Soft surrender.
Just mute survival.

On his wall, a line:
"What does not hum, does not call."
No one heard him go.

<u>Silence</u>

Silence is no empty room,
no void where whispers cease;
it gathers shadows, blooms,
and holds the aching peace.

It's not the end but breath,
a quiet space to grieve
a moment stretched like death,
a chance to just believe.

The world withdraws its song,
and stillness lays its claim;
in silence, we belong
to loss without a name.

The Couple Who Labeled the Stars

They traced the sky with trembling hands,
a soft chalk bloom on the windowpane.
Each star a secret only they could understand,
a map of moments drawn in fading flame.

A soft chalk bloom on the windowpane,
their whispered names drifted into the night.
A map of moments drawn in fading flame,
constellations born from their shared light.

Their whispered names drifted into the night,
like promises whispered between the dark.
Constellations born from their shared light,
small beacons kindling a fragile spark.

Like promises whispered between the dark,
each breath a tether, each glance a vow.
Small beacons kindling a fragile spark
they lingered where silence would not allow.

Each breath a tether, each glance a vow,
they traced the sky with trembling hands.
They lingered where silence would not allow,
a soft chalk bloom on the windowpane.

Listen

                                    to the

                    sky

The Girl Who Took Off Her Shoes

She left her shoes at water's edge,
lined neatly on the mossy stone,
as quiet as a whispered pledge,
no footprints where she'd walked alone.

The pool lay still, no ripple stirred,
a glassy mirror holding skies,
not one sound, not one soft word,
beneath the silence of her eyes.

No signs of struggle, no sharp cries,
just empty space where she had been,
the calm that follows lullabies,
and secrets locked in quiet skin.

Barefoot, she walked beyond the reach,
beyond the world, beyond the hue
a silent lesson she would teach:
sometimes the path is just to lose.

The night wrapped round her like a veil,
soft shadows breathed along the shore,
the stars alone would tell the tale
of footsteps never heard once more.

Her shoes remained, untouched, pristine,
a quiet question left behind
where had she gone, what had she seen,
what peace did she hope to find?

And in the stillness, something spoke,
a gentle sigh, a distant hum,
the earth itself began to cloak
the girl who chose to quietly come.

The Archivist

They say the Archivist stands apart,
a quiet ghost behind the shelves of time,
recording endings, stories torn apart,
but never writing verse or rhyme.

No name, no face, no whispered clue,
just ink and paper folded neat,
a silent witness, always true,
to every loss and each defeat.

Perhaps they know who penned these lines
the ones you read with bated breath
a keeper of the fading signs,
a scribe who watches life and death.

The Archivist himself leaves no trace,
only the echo of others' grace.

The Quiet Road

In shadows deep, where silence takes its throne,
The ones who laid their weary bodies down,
Have taught us all to bear loss on our own.

Not all who face the night will wear a crown.
Some fold themselves like maps too vast to roam,
And choose a softer peace instead of frown.

They step aside, where darkness feels like home,
Not weakness, but a grief too sharp to name,
A stillness where no blood or fear will comb.

Their stories flicker, none are quite the same,
A choir singing songs beyond our reach,
A whispered echo carved in quiet flame.

The world may end, but memories will teach
That courage comes in many fragile ways
In silent rooms, in hands that never breach.

Though gates may fall and fires burn the day,
There is a strength in choosing to let go,
In bending where the breaking seems to stay.

The quiet ones who turn away from woe,
Who fold their hands, who close their weary eyes,
Still hold a light we only dare to know.

Their silence speaks beyond the last goodbyes,
A testament to battles lost and quelled,
To love that neither time nor death denies.

The breath that lingers when the voice is stilled,
The gentle pulse beneath the heavy dark,
Are traces of the souls who once fulfilled

The roles of hope and love, a fragile spark
That flickers on, beyond the touch of fear,
A quiet place where broken dreams embark.

Not all who fade are lost, nor disappear
They hold the spaces no one dares to fill,
And teach us how to grieve without despair.

So hold their stories close, remember still
The ones who chose to walk the silent road,
Who bowed beneath a fate too sharp to kill.

Their steps may vanish under winter's load,
But in their absence, something yet remains:
A whispered truth, a solace softly owed.

The end is never truly where hope wanes
It lives in every breath, in every choice,
In those who bear the weight of heavy chains,

The Hollowing

The smoke has no direction now.
The names are heat that cannot hold.
What isn't burned is bowed or breaking.
Even silence smells like something old.

The fire didn't end with smoke.
It ended with no one calling for help.
I walked for three days and saw no eyes.
Only open doors.
Only silence that used to be names.

I've stayed beneath the hill where fire spread,
just far enough to count the silent dead.

The walls are gone, but some things still remain
a scent, a shoe, a doorframe scorched by flame.

I walk the edge and do not speak out loud.
Some ashes still believe they are a crowd.

I mark the paths where others fled too fast,
and trace the outlines memory makes last.

A fence half-fallen points toward something true:
the end was not a cliff, just something through.

I've found that waiting teaches what won't leave,
and what we touch when all we do is grieve.

So I remain. I listen through the steam.
The world is quiet. That does not mean it's clean.

And when the sky remembers how to turn,
I'll walk again. Once grief forgets to burn.

Canto VII – Ash Moves Slowly

The wind forgot which way the gates had blown.
The sky looked down and saw too much to weep.
The ground fell soft, like someone left alone.

A chair sat upright where the flames ran deep.
The table near it held a single ring.
The beds were black. The shoes were stacked in sleep.

I moved through what was left not witnessing,
just breathing where the memory unspooled.
The light still fell, but did not do a thing.

A scorched tarp flapped. A hallway stayed half-cooled.
The names on doors had blurred into the walls.
A doll was found, its cloth mouth loosely ruled.

I do not call these ruins, only stalls
the kind of pause the world forgets to break.
A silence split by nothing but its scrawls.

A spoon still lay beside a melted plate.
A note was pinned to glass: We are not here.
I read it once, then left it to its fate.

A girl's red shoes were placed too close, too near.
A bunk was burned, but not entirely through.
The shadows on the wall refused to clear.

A boot was filled with seeds no one knew.
A garden grew behind a shattered van.
A branch was tied with thread, in pink and blue.

The road was cracked, but knew just how to span
the distance from before to something thin.
The path was gone, but still it somehow ran.

A bag was torn beside the clinic bin.
Its contents spilled some gauze, a name tag: Lee.
A prayer was scrawled across a bottle's skin.

Forgive me, God. Or let me cease to be.
The cap was off. The liquid long since gone.
The flame had stopped. But left behind debris.

A church still stood, but only with one song
still echoing from where the choir once stood.
The pews were ash. The hymn too short, too wrong.

A child's chair remained near where it should,
but nothing else recalled its matching set.
The crayon line stopped just before the wood.

I watched a door swing once, then still, then set.
The hinges sighed. The wind moved on its own.
A teacup waited, full, without regret.

A street sign bent, its meaning overthrown.
It read slow down in letters scorched and gray.
A mirror faced a wall and sat alone.

I passed no ghosts, but knew they saw my way.
I touched no walls, but heard them in my pace.
The smoke had thinned. But still, it did not stray.

A radio was found, but not its case.
It played one note and then it died again.
Its tone became the shape of empty space.

A record spun with no stylus or pen.
A chair turned slowly toward a half-gone view.
A child's toy blinked, then never blinked again.

I do not know what else there was to do.
The wind had carried all that tried to stay.
And still, I walked as I was meant to do.

I did not bury. I did not delay.
I simply walked the paths that grief had drawn
not back, not forward, but a ghost half-way.

And in the hush, the air still called me on.
The hollow does not echo just responds.

Objects in Place

The sink still drips.
The rug is clean.

The fire passed here
but didn't explain.
One shoe under the table.
A fork beside it.

No dust.
No burn.

A window cracked but not broken.
The air inside is untouched,
like someone left mid-sentence.

Like they'll return
once the silence gets tired.

The rooms were still, their breath too faint to claim.
The fork, the shoe, each ghost without a name.

I walked through silence thick with soot and thread,
Expecting rot, not roots that bloom instead.

The fire had passed, but not all things had fled.
One leaf held light. One vine refused the dead.

I felt no joy. No triumph shaped my path.
Just quiet, curling through the fire's aftermath.

I do not know who planted, knelt, or prayed
but something green had grown where none had stayed.

The Greenhouse

I came upon it behind what used to be a school, half-buried in vines. Its roof was fractured in places, but enough glass held that warmth still gathered. Inside, the air was heavier than outside not with rot, but with something like expectation.
Rows of greens pressed upward in trays: wilted, yes, but still reaching. There were no tools. No footprints. Just moss-soft silence and one overturned watering can. I wondered who had come here last. Did they leave in fear? Were they taken mid-task? Or did they believe the plants could outlive them? Some leaves had curled into themselves. Others seemed to stretch, greedy for light. One stalk of basil had flowered. There was no sound except for a slow drip from the broken roof, like time refusing to stop altogether.

I did not touch the plants. I bowed my head.

broken windowpane
the basil reaches upward
as if it still prays

The Garden That Was Spared

Beyond the scorch, where fences bowed in heat,
I found a gate unbent; its hinges clean.
No wreckage, no bones, no blood beneath my feet
just soft soil and petals edged in green.

A row of lilies leaned as if in prayer.
A vine climbed slow around a rusted rake.
No footsteps marked the path to show who cared
yet all was tended, living, wide awake.

I bent to touch a bloom. My hand held back.
Too much of me was fire, or smoke, or doubt.
This place had missed the maps. Had slipped the track.
The world forgot to claim it on the route.

I left no mark. Just silence where I knelt
a moment not for pain, but what I felt.

Rooftop Chairs

The stairwell was blocked, but I climbed anyway. Up four levels of wind-split concrete and graffiti that meant nothing now. The top of the parking garage gave no answers, just sky.

That's where I found them: two plastic chairs, faded red, turned toward the horizon. One had a cracked back. The other still bore the imprint of someone's coat. The shape of waiting, or retreat. Between them sat a bottle, empty, clean, upright. There was no glass nearby. No crumbs. No mess. Just presence.

I imagined two people watching the end arrive together. Not with panic, but in the way people once watched fireworks or dusk. No signs of a struggle. No signs they left at all.

And that's the strange thing: I've seen chaos, fire, rooms of clawed doors. But this stillness made me ache. Because I think they thought they were safe. Or maybe they were. Just not in the way we measure safety anymore.

no voices remain
only the way chairs were placed
to speak with the sky

I've passed through towns too silent for a name,
and learned what loss leaves when it burns the frame.

These are the things not buried, not reclaimed
the remnants not remembered, just unnamed.

I write them now, not so they won't be gone
but so you'll know what people left turned on.

What Was Left

- A single shoe, child-sized, waterlogged
- A wedding dress in a plastic bag
- Half a rosary melted into pavement
- Ten unopened letters marked *Urgent*
- The smell of soup, long gone, sealed in a pressure pot
- A toothbrush still foaming in the sink
- Two cereal boxes. One empty, one sealed
- Keys in a lock that no longer turns
- The phrase "Back Soon" in lipstick on a mirror
- Shoelaces tied tight with no feet in them
- A crossword missing the final word
- One pink rain boot beneath a church pew
- A birdcage with the door open
- A box of pictures, faces blurred by heat
- A page of music scorched at the refrain.
- A doorframe with tally marks carved down the side
- Six stuffed animals lined up like they were waiting
- One jacket, zipped and ready
- Three bullets left in a sock drawer
- A guitar string snapped mid-note
- Two chairs facing a black screen
- A bag of rice with a single tear
- A music box that won't close
- A photo taped to a fence: *"She is loved."*
- The smell of someone still trying to stay
- A mirror turned to face the wall
- A pacifier beside a jar of coins
- A journal with every page torn out but one
- A cracked phone still buzzing every hour

- A chessboard mid-game, both kings gone
- One glove in the freezer
- A radio locked on static
- A prayer written in red on the wall
- A candle that melted but never lit
- A couch turned barricade, still warm
- A scarf tied to a doorknob

I wrote them down not just for what they meant,
but for the silence stamped in each event.

Echoes of the Forgotten

The wind laments through hollowed bones of trees,
A dirge for souls that wandered far from grace.
Their whispers carried on the autumn breeze.

The sun, a sallow eye in pallid face,
Peers down upon the remnants of the land,
Illuminating death's cold, stark embrace.

Once vibrant fields now yield to lifeless sand,
Where laughter's echo fades into the dust,
And hope slips through the cracks like grains unplanned.

A church stands crooked, steeple turned to rust,
Its bells long silenced by the weight of sin,
Its pews now home to creatures void of trust.

The stained glass saints, their colors worn and thin,
Cast fractured rainbows on the blood-stained floor,
Their halos dimmed, their faces stretched in grin.

A child's doll lies beside the open door,
Its eyes plucked out, its smile a jagged seam,
A relic of the innocence left in the before.

The air is thick with rot, a long lost dream,
Where every breath invites the stench of death,
And shadows dance within the smoky gleam.

A figure moves with neither pulse nor breath,
Its limbs contorted in a ghastly pose,
A marionette of fate, devoid of depth.

Its eyes, two voids where once did light impose,
Now mirrors to the darkness deep within,
Reflecting all the pain the world bestows.

It reaches out with hands of pallid skin,
Each finger tipped with nails of blackened glass,
To touch the living, draw their spirits in.

The living flee, their footsteps swift to pass,
Yet echoes of their screams remain behind,
A symphony of sorrow none surpass.

Among the ruins, madness intertwines,
A tapestry of grief and shattered minds,
Where sanity dissolves in twisted lines.

The moon ascends, its glow a pale disguise,
Revealing truths the daylight dares not show,
Unmasking all the terror in the skies.

Beneath its gaze, the dead begin to grow,
Emerging from the soil with silent cries,
Their hunger driving them to overthrow.

They march in cadence, void of mortal ties,
A legion of the lost, their purpose clear:
To feast upon the world that let them die.

The living cower, gripped by primal fear,
Their weapons futile against death's decree,
Their prayers unanswered, falling on deaf ear.

A mother weeps beside a withered tree,
Her child clutched tight, a shield against the night,
Yet shadows creep where light no longer be.

The child stirs, its eyes a ghastly sight,
Once blue, now clouded with a milky haze,
Its breath a hiss, its grip a deadly bite.

The mother's scream ascends in mournful praise,
A lullaby to those who roam the dark,
A testament to love that death betrays.

In alleyways where silence leaves its mark,
The rats have fled, the vermin sense the doom,
Their absence speaks of horrors that embark.

A man stands tall amidst the city's gloom,
His eyes alight with fire, his blade in hand,
Defiant in the face of certain tomb.

He fights not for the glory or the land,
But for the memory of days gone by,
For dreams that crumble into grains of sand.

Each swing a verse, each strike a battle cry,
A poem etched in blood upon the street,
A sonnet to the will that won't comply.

But even heroes' hearts can cease to beat,
And as he falls, the darkness claims its due,
His legacy a tale of grim defeat.

The city sleeps beneath a crimson hue,
Its dreams consumed by nightmares come to life,
Its streets a canvas painted with the rue.

Yet in the depths, amid the endless strife,
A spark persists, a flicker in the shade,
A whisper of the ever-dying life.

A child hums tunes her mother once had played,
Her voice a beacon in the choking dark,
A melody that will not be dismayed.

The dead pause, stirred by this ethereal mark,
Their heads inclined, as if to hear the song,
A moment's peace within the endless stark.

But hunger reigns, the silence doesn't prolong,
They surge anew, the lullaby ignored,
The child alone amidst the ghastly throng.

Yet in her eyes, a light the dark abhorred,
A flame that even death could not eclipse,
A hope that life and love might be restored.

The Music Room

The door was already open. A melted brass knob, a scorch mark above the frame. The fire had passed through, but it hadn't stayed. It left behind only one message: this mattered once.

Inside: a piano with half its keys gone. The rest charred but holding shape. Sheet music still clung to the corkboard, curled and blackened at the edges. I could still read the notes. Adagio. D minor. For two hands. The kind of piece played at dusk, or just before the storm.

The bench was cracked. Someone had tried to sit, even as the heat came. I pictured them playing anyway. Fingers trembling, sweat mixing with ash, the melody never finished.

I reached out and touched the wood. It was cold. Not a single key made sound. And yet I heard something in my mind. Not the song. The moment before it.

When breath is held. When the hands hover.

even in ruin
the silence holds its posture
every note unstruck

I left the room where silence held its tune,
where keys unplayed still echoed through the ruin.

But outside sound began to stretch and bend
not music, no, but voices that pretend

to teach, to pray, to warn, to memorize
their hymns made not from faith, but compromise.

I followed chalk lines scrawled in ash and thread,
each one a path toward what the brave had said.

Schools all burned but still hold the wise.
The songs are softer now, but still they rise.

The Last Schools and Shrines

One school remained with desks still thick in dust.
Its globe lay cracked, its chalk a brittle line.
The flags were gone. The windows leached with rust.

The children sat in rows but gave no sign
of age or grade they learned what they could keep.
The teacher spoke in rhyme, a quiet spine.

She said, "Our lessons now are fire and sleep.
The test is when to run, not when to write.
The grades are grief. The rules are buried deep."

The blackboard bore a single word: recite.
And all the students whispered it in turn.
Their pencils sharpened not for math but fight.

A girl once sang a lullaby she'd learned
before the Fall, before the sky had cracked.
She wept mid-note. The silence did not burn.

The floor had maps of cities now attacked.
Each one was labeled Was or Nevermore.
A globe spun slowly, names already sacked.

Outside the gym, a banner Do Not War
had been revised with ash and broken glass:
Do Not Forget What We Were Fighting For.

They built a shrine beside the stairwell's pass
not to a god, but to a boy who wrote
the alphabet in blood before his last.

His name was Ben. They kept his paper coat
and hung it like a flag of sacred thread.
They found his final poem in his throat.

It read: If I am lost, I'm not yet dead.
And every child had carved those words in stone.
They murmured them before they broke their bread.

The teachers didn't preach. They stood alone
with eyes that saw too much, too young, too raw.
They'd once been taught. Now they were flesh and bone.

One nun took guard with what remained of law.
She held a cricket bat and spoke in verse.
Her Psalms were torn and stitched to fit the flaw.

They held a mass each week beside the hearse
made out of chairs, with ribbons for a hood.
They prayed with laughter, quiet, or a curse.

The altar held a box of water, wood,
a stuffed bear missing eyes, a candle stub.
One child confessed he'd never understood

why saints were burned but still they called it love.
The nun said, "Fire's what makes memory stay."
She kissed his brow. He smiled. She called him dove.

Another shrine was found beneath decay
a bunker turned into a sacred hall.
They lit old flashlights as their Milky Way.

Each light was named for one who could not crawl
away in time, or chose to guard the door.
They blinked in code across the concrete wall.

One shrine was just a tree no longer sore.
Its branches held a dozen notes in string.
They flapped like tongues that needed one word more.

The scribbles told of birthdays, faith, and spring.
One said: We made it through, and that was all.
One said: Forgive me for what silence brings.

And I, the poet, knelt beside the wall.
I read aloud what others tried to save.
I felt the air grow deep, grow wide, grow tall.

I wrote their lines into a hidden cave
The world may fall but still, the stories crave.

Quiet Moments

There are places
where fire does not consume
it only reminds.
I stood where echoes
curl like smoke
around broken rafters.

Not everything burns.
Some things settle.
A teacup upright in the ruin,
the outline of a fern
on scorched wallpaper,
the heel mark of a child in soot.

These are not signs.
They are pauses.
They are how memory breathes
when breath is no longer there.

And what I carried
from the music room
was not the song
but the hush that waits
to be chosen.

The Last Garden

No gate.
No path.
Just green.

A meadow where a grocery used to be.
Peonies in a checkout lane.
Ferns spilling from the deli counter.

Silence, but not emptiness.
Bees hum where sirens used to scream.
Roots split the linoleum like old arguments.

I walked through it barefoot.
Not by choice
the vines took my shoes.

There were no signs to read,
no names carved into benches.

But I knew where I stood.

This was the last garden.
Not planted,
but promised.

Not made by mercy,
but by rot.

The ground was soft with memory.
The blossoms leaned into my breath.

I did not pick a single flower.
I do not think they were meant for me.

Some things grow only
after we leave.

The Road Beyond Sound

I stayed longer than I meant to.
That's what silence does.
It wraps around the ribs,
turns into breath,
then into gravity.

I stopped counting days.
I stopped looking at the sky.
There was no danger, not anymore.
Not here.

The dead had thinned, or gone still.
Whatever moved now was wind, memory,
or me.
Sometimes I imagined voices through the walls.
But when I stepped closer, there was only dust and frost.

I saw a boy's shoe on a fence post.
A trail of books without covers.
A handprint in soot on the side of a truck.
Every sign whispered the same message:
someone made it this far.
No one stayed.

This morning, I boiled water.
Wrote nothing.
Then I packed what I had and stood beside the road.
It's not that I believe in next.
It's that I know how not to stop.

*the dust does not ask
if the foot that passed was yours
it just takes the shape*

Ghosts of Memory

I woke and could not name the month or day.
The sun had set in colors I'd not known.
The trees looked changed, or maybe I'd just frayed.

A song I'd once adored had lost its tone.
Its melody dissolved inside my head.
The words returned as dust, not flesh or bone.

I traced a name I thought my father said.
It ended halfway through and would not mend.
I tried to rhyme it, but the line was dead.

I found a box I buried for a friend.
It held old notes, a photo, and one pin.
But when I read them, none could comprehend.

Some memories returned, but wrong within.
My mother's voice now whispered someone else.
My school was placed in lands I've never been.

One day I named the sky, and lost myself.
The word collapsed and curled behind my tongue.
I wept not from the loss but from the stealth.

I built a wall of all I'd once been young
to hold a sock, a coin, a line of prayer.
But each grew strange, as if from someone flung.

A man I met had ribbons in his hair.
He tied one each time he forgot a face.
His scalp was full. He smiled without despair.

I found a girl who labeled every space.
She marked the trees, the wind, the curve of ash.
She said, "If I remember, I'm not erased."

A child wore names as beads in ragged sash.
Each color meant a moment she could feel.
She dropped one when the memory would crash.

And me I wrote on walls to make things real.
I rhymed the cracks, the echoes, and the light.
I used each verse to tether thought and meal.

One night I dreamed in letters lost to sight.
I wrote them down, but all the vowels were wrong.
The consonants refused to hold them tight.

A woman sang, "Remembering makes us strong."
But each refrain grew thinner in her throat.
Her second verse was silence far too long.

One boy drew faces just to help him note
the friends he'd had, or maybe just believed.
He sketched their smiles in charcoal on his coat.

A girl said, "Memory can't be retrieved
it grows like fungus in the quiet mind."
She scraped her thoughts like bark from what deceived.

I carved the phrase be kind and tried to bind
it to a place, a year, a single deed.
It slipped like smoke. The shape refused to wind.

We made new words when old ones wouldn't lead.
We called the stars the quiet burning skin.
We named our grief the hunger that can plead.

A woman taught a class of seven kin
to write with colors drawn from moss and heat.
They spelled their names in shapes, not ink or tin.

One wrote a spiral when he tried to greet.
One traced a feather every time he lied.
One stitched her story on her moving feet.

And I, the poet, watched as minds defied
the clock, the mirror, and the hollow name.
I wrote not truth, but what the mind implied.

Each stanza now was both a spark and frame
to catch the fall, to pin what might be lost.
A line, a word, a whisper kept from flame.

you're still

breathing

let that

be enough

I thought all speech had vanished into dust,
that pages curled to bone, that ink grew rust.

But silence isn't void, it's just delay.
It waits for those who do not look away.

Where ruins slept, I found a hidden seam:
a stair of books half-buried in a beam.

I knelt among the fragments, dared to read
the echo of a grammar stitched in seed.

One shelf still bore the shape of ancient thought.
Its letters sang of truths the fire forgot.

A scroll of myths, a map of vanished stars,
a poem bound in thread and softened scars.

Not everything was lost. Some things were shelved
by hands that hoped the future might be delved.

I do not know what all these symbols mean,
but even unread wisdom keeps us clean.

So let this be the breath before the lore,
the hush that parts the ash to show a door.

Archives of the Unspoken

We thought
the archives would remember for us
all the names, all the warnings.
But even ink has a threshold.

Words broke
like glass too long in frost.
Some curled
into shapes no tongue could hold.

But language is brittle
when it forgets its breath.

Now, we read silence
the way we once read scripture
with reverence, and regret.

Where the Roots Sing

Beneath the ash and the echo,
past the cracked train tracks
and the playground's rusting bones,

the roots have gathered.

Not to strangle.
Not to heal.
But to sing what we forgot.

A music that moves through marrow.
Low and patient.
Without need for air.

I pressed my ear to the earth once.
Thought I heard thunder.
But it was memory.

They carry what we dropped
lullabies, blood-hymns,
a cradle hum heard in the marrow.
The earth remembers what we could not hold.

Lullabies swallowed whole.
Screams softened into syllables.
Names rubbed smooth as stone.

They do not sing for us.
They sing because they must.

The soil has no mouth.
But the roots remember the tune.

And when I lie down for the last time,
I hope they find me.

If I lie down beside them,
they will remember my shape.
Not with words, but with rhythm.
A pulse. A hush. A hum.

I hope they remember my shape
and make a sound of it.

The Anatomy of the Dead V

The eyes do not rot.
They glaze.
Like windows no longer cleaned,
but still open.

They follow movement, not emotion.

When a match is struck,
they blink.
When a hand is raised,
they flinch.

Not recognition. Only reaction.

They do not know you.
But they remember
what it felt like to be known.

Some still weep,
but salt has no memory.

Just the shape of loss
without the weight.

The pupils stay wide
not in fear,
but to let in whatever is left
of the world.

The Buried Cities

The cities moaned beneath a dust-swept skin.
Their lungs were vents, their hearts were boiler rooms.
They wheezed through steel, through silence grown within.

I passed beneath a sign that read Costumes
half-gone, the word now just cost and a blank.
The mannequins had melted into tombs.

One alley reeked of sulfur, blood, and rank.
Its shops were husks of thread and fire-charred lace.
A pram lay overturned beside a bank.

A dome collapsed to frame a central place
where someone burned old textbooks in a ring.
The ash had left a handprint on the base.

I crossed a stage where pigeons tried to sing.
Their cries were hollow fugues in broken key.
A single spotlight flickered on its string.

A metro card was pinned to memory
beneath a statue missing both its arms.
Its nameplate simply said: Nowhere to Be.

In one cafe I saw old tech's alarms
a cash screen blinking endlessly declined.
A chair still rocked, as if beneath old charms.

And there, among the shadows, vines entwined
a bus stop where a poem had been tagged:
We mattered once. But history went blind.

The glass still bore the blood of words unbagged.
One message read: Don't enter the museum.
Inside, the floors were cracked, the portraits lagged.

I found a map inside a mausoleum.
It showed the zones of silence marked in red.
Its ink was smeared with what I guessed was serum.

A phone booth stood. Its roof had long been shed.
Inside, someone had scratched the phrase: Just Call.
And though it rang, no dial tone had bled.

A church bell hung in place but did not fall.
Its rope had frayed into a hundred threads.
Its altar still had shoes lined by the wall.

One hallway bore a trail of blinking reds
emergency signs looping without end.
A screen declared: Evacuation Spreads.

I passed a tower titled To Ascend.
Its stairs were melted. Half the walls had bowed.
Its windows watched but could not recommend.

A library had died beneath a load
of ceilings crashed and manuscripts in rain.
One page read Dear then broke in ink and code.

A voice looped on an intercom in vain:
Please exit left... please exit left... and faded.
I followed it, as if it might explain.

The streets were filled with echoes long outdated.
I swore I heard a child call out a rhyme
but silence came, too quick, too automated.

I wandered past a theater out of time.
Its screen showed stars, or what the reels had kept.
Its rows were graveyard pews turned out of line.

One billboard screamed, We laughed, we burned, we slept.
Its bulbs all shattered, yet the slogan stayed
a final truth the living never prepped.

And me, the poet, knelt where buildings swayed
and traced a haiku into molten wire:
Ash remembers sound that once obeyed.

Each tower seemed to whisper: Now retire.
Each chamber hummed with static, not with ghosts.
Each stairwell asked me, "What do you require?"

I wrote one stanza on a post of posts
a bulletin where flyers curled like skin.
Its ink said: For the poet, not the hosts.

I left a line where bus seats once had been:
We rode together, though the world grew thin.
And left that city with the hope within.

The towers fell, but some doors stayed aligned.
Beneath the rust, the roots of thought entwined.

Where silence pressed its thumb into the stone,
A whisper grew where no one walked alone.

Not all was ash some voices chose to wait,
Beneath the weight of flame, they sealed the gate.

The city broke, but memory found a seam.
Descent begins where ruins start to dream.

Archive Beneath the Earth

Below a shattered library's collapsed dome,
I found a stair disguised in marble dust.
It spiraled down through quiet, ash, and loam.

The walls were lined with mold and caked with rust.
I lit a match; the air was thick and old.
Each step I took, the silence begged, "Entrust."

I reached a door with panels split and cold.
Its surface bore a sigil Preserve All.
I knocked once, twice. No answer did unfold.

I pushed and entered what had once held sprawl
of servers, drives, and endless glowing code.
Now dark, now still the kingdom's final fall.

The shelves were ranked like pews in some abode.
I passed a row of disks in glassy case,
their labels smudged, their titles long erode.

A paper note read: Memory's Last Place.
I opened drawers, and found a folder thin
its contents: just one printed line and trace.

The line said Speak, or silence takes it in.
I touched the keyboard once, expecting none
but pixels blinked, like ghost returned to skin.

A screen lit up. A voice as pale as sun
asked softly, "Poet, why have you arrived?"
I said, "To mark what war and ash undone."

"Input accepted," said the vault contrived.
"Begin with name." I paused. I'd long forgot.
"I am the one who watched and then survived."

I typed not facts, but places where we fought
a plaza full of shoes, a pond of hair.
A prayer scratched in a boot, a child's plot.

I typed of zones where hope grew thin as air.
I logged the jokes, the oaths, the ways we tricked.
The screen said Saved, though no one else was there.

One box held books all printed for the fix
of post-world data: How to Bury Sky,
What Crows Recall, The Plague in Forty Tricks.

I left my name on each. I did not lie.
I wrote a stanza in the folder's face:
We ended slow. The stars had stopped to try.

I carved a final line in steel with grace:
The world forgets, but language makes its tomb.
Then sealed the drawer, no tears, no last embrace.

And as I left, I passed one screen still bloom
it flickered words I had not typed or known:
Thank you, poet. You returned the room.

Some scripts were sung in moss, some carved in shell.
Not all that's buried fades, and not all fell.

We walked through glyphs the wind could not erase
Each root a sentence tied to some lost place.

Beneath it all, the breath of codes remained,
And language hummed through steel and systems drained.

Then someone wrote a poem in the dust.
And that was when the room began to trust.

Alphabet of Bone

They made letters from memory.
Not from lines or curves, but from gestures:
a cupped hand meant wait.
A finger across lips meant remember.
Two palms open
and raised meant we saw it too.
Ash gathered on the floor
became the page.
Sticks became pens. Fire was the ink.

A child spelled her name
by tying knots in thread.
A man marked days
by carving the sound of each breath into bone.
None of it translated, but all of it endured.

They called it the Newalphabet.
No vowels. No promises.
Only the letters that survived.

The Language of Dust

The tongue of dust still speaks in seams and grout.
A syllable of soot on shattered tile.
A whisper hangs in pipes that once rang out
ghost consonants that echo for a mile.

A syllable of soot on shattered tile,
where signs once said: Come Home or Please Don't Leave.
Ghost consonants that echo for a mile,
the grammar smudged in rust, in hope, in grief.

Where signs once said: Come Home or Please Don't Leave,
I brushed a sentence from a locker door
the grammar smudged in rust, in hope, in grief
a verse in red that named what was before.

I brushed a sentence from a locker door.
The tongue of dust still speaks in seams and grout.
A verse in red that named what was before.
A whisper hangs in pipes that once rang out.

They catalogued the wars with threadbare ink,
And taught lost verbs the way a people think.

Each symbol, trace, and syllable once meant
A world before the quiet took consent.

The letters, half-erased, still held their cry
The sounds we lose are those that learned to lie.

The archive breathes in pauses, not in lore;
To name a thing is how we mark a door.

The Archivist's Room

The room was locked from the inside.
No guard. No warning.
Just a crack in the stone wall,
as if the building had exhaled once
and left a breath behind.

The door was scorched,
but the hinges shone.
Inside, the dust was different
it lay deliberate,
like lace placed on a mourning table.

Shelves lined the walls in patient rows,
each labeled in a hand so fine
it felt whispered more than written.

Section A: Before Names.
Section C: Cartographies of Mistake.
Section F: Final Fires, First Prayers.

One shelf held only books
with burned corners,
spines still strong.

Another, just blank journals, s
tacked like unopened questions.
One volume was labeled simply:
Forgiveness

In the corner
a cot made perfectly,
edges tucked like someone
hadn't yet earned rest.

Beside it:
a chipped mug,
a broken pair of glasses
resting on a page that read:

"We keep language
so it can keep us.
Even when we forget what we mean."

The air was warm,
not from heat,
but from memory.
You could feel it in your teeth.

A row of tuning forks
lay beneath a cloth
each tagged with a name,
as though someone meant
to tune the world back
to how it used to sound.

There was no body.
No bones.
Just a long scarf folded over a chair,
a half-used candle,
and one list tacked above the desk:

Words no longer safe
Metaphors banned for cruelty
Phrases used too often at the end

On the floor, beneath a loose plank:
a metal box filled
with children's drawings,
a letter addressed
To the Future,
and one final stanza in trembling ink:

"If the world forgets the shape of breath,
this is how we spelled it
not in fire,
but in the pause before we lit the match."

Found on Magnetic Tape

The reel-to-reel still ticked beneath the ash,
a ribbon wound in static, hum, and heat.
I played it, knowing risk, and feared the crash
but then: a voice, too young, too clear, too sweet.

"Today we learned that fire can forget,"
she said, "but stories burn a different way.
"A teacher coughed. A metronome was set.
Then laughter. Chalk. The lessons for the day.

Another clip a wedding in the rain.
A recipe recited soft and sure
A lullaby from someone lost to pain.
A speech: "We will endure, no, not just endure."

I wound it back, and wrote in trembling pen:
We are the voices longing to begin.

The tape had stopped, but something stayed in air
a voice too brave to vanish in despair.

It hummed inside the hollows of my chest,
a rhythm not of fear, but of request.

"Go," it seemed to say, "the ruins still await.
Bring words to where the silence learned its weight."

Where towers wept, I'd carve a verse in steel.
Where children played, I'd etch what scars still feel.

Where fires danced, I'd stitch a rhyme in soot,
and leave behind a stanza near each root.

The graves of sound. The temples scorched with lore.
The shelters swept. The rusted market floor.

Each landmark claimed by time, by ash, by war
I'd gift a line, then step through one step more.

For memory is not what fades, but stays
when someone dares to write inside the blaze.

I set my pen where monuments once rose
to be the ink that even ruin knows.

Pilgrimage of Ink

I left the vault and walked through fields of wire.
Each fencepost hummed with echoes of a scream.
Each pylon held the residue of fire.

I wrapped my poems in cloth and brittle seam.
Each one was sealed with wax and pressed with stone.
They weren't commands, just breath inside a dream.

At every town, I left behind a bone
of stanza shaped to match the earth it found.
No rhymes for kings, no myths for golden throne.

One ruined school became a burial mound.
I placed a haiku carved into a desk:
The bell rang once. Then silence wrapped the sound.

In what was once a church, now statuesque,
I etched a psalm in candle wax and soot.
The pews had all been stacked in holy wreck.

Beside a gas pump, by a melted foot
of plastic deer, I left a villanelle
about the nights we prayed but could not look.

In cities drowned in moss, I chose to dwell
a moment more, then pressed a sonnet flat
between two bricks beside a broken well.

I found a door with symbols where it sat
a hospital turned garden of regret.
Its wall became my verse's sacred mat.

One courtyard bore the remnants of a pet
a collar tied to branches with some thread.
I left a lyric there so none forget.

Some poems I threw from towers overhead.
They caught the breeze like dying paper birds.
Their titles: Why We Stayed, The Book of Bread.

I met a man who dealt in traded words.
He sold me silence, priced in salted tears.
I paid in meter, gave him borrowed verbs.

I walked until the mountains had no years.
The trees stood older than our myths of war.
I nailed a quatrain to a cedar's spears.

It read: This voice is neither less nor more.
It's just the thread you hold before the night.
Then let it go where pages can't restore.

I wrote a rhyme on backs of traffic light
the green was gone, the red still faintly glowed.
The middle flickered dimmer every night.

Each time I stopped, I planted what I owed
not stories vast, but moments built in sand.
One read: He knelt before the last upload.

Another verse was buried near a hand
still holding chalk beside a broken wall.
It read: We taught ourselves not to disband.

In coastal towns where waves began to crawl
into the homes, I left my lines on shells.
They echoed with the quiet of it all.

One cave I entered smelled of dust and wells.
Its walls were soft with soot from ancient fire.
I wrote: Our thoughts became the fox's spells.

I passed a place where someone strung a lyre
made out of spokes and copper strands of grief.
I tied a poem there and called it Choir.

And I, the poet, moved like autumn leaf
not swift, but with a purpose in the drift.
Each verse I left was not to end, but to brief.

<u>On a Collapsing Overpass (etched into concrete)</u>

"The Bridge Between"

Where wheels once roared, now grasses speak.

A single line: be strong, not sleek.

This stone has heard both vow and groan

I write for those who walked alone.

<u>On a Broken Circuit Panel (scrawled in graphite)</u>

"Syntax After Fire"

If you decode this final spark,

remember light can glitch the dark.

No power now, no clean command

just ghosted code from human hand.

On the Back of a Museum Frame (carved with nail)

"The Exhibit Is Memory"

The label's gone. The art, a blur.

But still, I write: they once were her.

Each brushstroke held a day, a breath

what time forgets, I guard from death.

<u>On a Tree at the Edge of the Crater (burned into bark)</u>

"Survivor Oak"

You lived through flame. So did this tree.

It does not speak, but shelters me.

I leave a line, not loud, not wide

But just enough to peek inside.

The Cartographer of Dust

I rose at dawn with nothing but a scroll,
my pen half-bent, my satchel lined with thread
a promise inked in hunger: mark each soul.

Where once a tower kept the clocks, I bled
a line of verse into the soot-stained wall,
then bowed to names the sirens left for dead.

A plaza cracked where pigeons used to brawl;
I knelt beneath the echo of a choir,
and left a rhyme that barely rose at all.

Near rusted rails and seats of broken wire,
I wrote for those who rode but didn't land,
whose breath had fed the engine's final fire.

Atop a school where children made their stand,
I carved a haiku in the bleached-out stone
its syllables too small to understand.

One mall remained, its mannequins alone,
their plastic hands still posed mid-point or pray.
I left a sonnet near the fashion zone.

A gas station still wept from yesterday;
I wrote a couplet in the pump's faint gleam,
about the cost of light and how we pay.

A chapel burned yet kept its ancient beam.
I sang a psalm inside the vacant nave,
then tucked a villanelle behind the seam.

Inside a vault not meant to house the brave,
I found an urn of names no one had kept.
I wrote a dirge for what I could not save.

One house had stood while all the others wept
its porch still swept, its mailbox gripped with rust.
There, on the screen door, I in silence slept.

I dreamed of those who named and did not trust
and of the once who once had been
and woke to scrawl a sestina in the dust.

Beneath a bridge, I met the ghosts of kin
who showed me where the bones began to crack.
I wrote a chant for silence thick as sin.

A sign still blinked: Last Shelter Out and Back.
I carved a line between each faded light
a guide for those who read the world in lack.

A mural bore a child mid-final flight,
her crayon wings undone by moss and mold.
I left a prayer she'd make it past the night.

In every alley where a truth was sold,
I marked the cost with just a single word.
Not sold in blood, nor silver, only cold.

Some places asked for songs they'd never heard;
I hummed, then left the lyrics out of reach.
What cannot be recalled must still be stirred.

A classroom where the blackboard used to teach
still held the date, though weathered into blur.
My chalk became the ghost of spoken speech.

I passed a bench beneath a holly spur,
where someone carved two names and then a third.
A poem bloomed before I could defer.

Each monument had once defied the herd
the empty tanks, the statues overgrown.
Each got a stanza, honest though absurd.

One soldier's helmet crowned a post alone.
I placed a ghazal there, each couplet raw
its rhymes like boots abandoned to the stone.

I found a drone entombed beneath a draw
and on its wing I inked a line of peace.
No code. No war. No logic. Just a flaw.

Near barricades now buried under fleece
of snow and ash and moss in equal claim,
I left a joke, a riddle without cease.

A playground bore no echo of a name,
but swings still swayed as if they held the breath
of games unplayed and joys that never came.

I wrote a rondeau there, defying death,
its looping form a shape the wind could keep
a rhythm passed from grieving into myth.

Atop a hill where no one came to weep,
I built a cairn of words I could not rhyme.
Some truths, you see, are simply sown too deep.

A fire hydrant stained with old red grime
still whispered water songs beneath the heat.
I left a spell to slow the burn of time.

Some shrines were crude just boots, or teeth, or meat
but even these I honored with my ink,
for not all heroes die with something neat.

A ferris wheel once turned upon the brink
and now stood still, its spokes the shape of grief.
I left a ballad at the lowest link.

A bunker held the echo of belief
inside, I scratched a line into the steel:
The poet sees. The world provides the thief.

A streetlamp buzzed. I knelt beneath its peel.
I placed a triolet inside its hum.
Its light was dull. But still, it tried to feel.

A garden grown in gas cans and in crumb
held lettuce soft and vines that split the stone.
I left a vow: We rise in where we're from.

And at the final place, I stood alone
a crater shaped like absence, not like war.
I took no notes. Just whispered to the bone.

I wrote no lines. I bowed, then left the floor.
For some things must be felt, not turned to lore.

I walked the vaults where vanished words were kept,
Where grammar cracked and consonants had wept.

Each book had teeth. Each scroll exhaled a sigh
The margins curled to speak, then chose to lie.

Ink bled like dusk through veils of skin,
And vowels forgot which mouths they once lived in.

I read a script that looped but did not end,
A prayer half-swallowed, meant to re-ascend.

The shelves were grave-marked lines the scribes betrayed,
Their footnotes stitched from meanings long decayed.

One lexicon was stitched with human hair
Its pages turned themselves, and did not care.

I left that place when language ceased to mourn,
When syntax curled like petals not yet born.

My boots were bruised with alphabets and ash,
The road ahead still humming static trash.

A sign half-buried read: FORGETTING CITY
and whispered it was beautiful, but not pretty.

So here I come, with notebook loose and torn,
To write the rites of those who can't be mourned.

They speak in breath. In silence. In decline.
They echo still and now their lines are mine.

Liturgies of the Unrested

They do not speak.
They repeat.

A bow, a breath,
a button placed where memory should be.

Here, forgetting is sacred.
Here, performance replaces prayer.

I do not write their stories.
I witness their loops.

<u>Processional</u>

I followed silence down a road of bone,
past signs in ash that turned their eyes from me,
each step repeating something not my own.

The sky was low. The wind forgot the sea.
A stage appeared, collapsed but standing still
its curtains torn in loops of elegy.

She stood alone, a girl with fractured will,
reciting songs the static never caught.
Each bow she made rewrote her final thrill.

A voice once bright now frayed by weathered thought
she sang of tomorrows that never came.
Her spotlight: firelight on the battles fought.

Then dusk gave form to one without a name,
a man who knelt where no one ever came near.
He whispered vows to shadows just the same.

His ring was ash, but worn with something clear
the shine of habit carved into the dusk.
He spoke as though a "yes" might still appear.

Then down an alley crowned in rust and musk
a boy danced circles round a shattered cake.
He smiled through teeth not meant to trust a husk.

He gave me buttons. Smoke. A toy to break.
He named the party guests who never showed.
His candles flickered inward for their sake.

I passed a table. Every plate bestowed
a name the mother spoke beneath her breath.
The chairs were full. The silence overflowed.

She served what grief had taught her after death
a folded napkin, hunger with no sound.
I left her hands mid-prayer, mid-spell, mid-wrath.

I sketched them all, their rituals unbound
by time or mercy stuck in reverent loop,
each action like a wound that won't be found.

And now I walk into the chapel's stoop,
where even breath must kneel and be unspoken.
A liturgy begins without a group.

Their plays persist, their final lines unbroken
not life, not death, but memory's token.

Tomorrow is my Turn to Shine

She stands alone where the cinders still cling.
Tomorrow is my turn to shine, she said.
Each word she speaks frays on a static string.

The boards beneath her blister, crack, and sing
the ghostly echo of a song long dead.
She stands alone where the cinders still cling.

Her bow is graceful, though the night won't bring
an audience beyond the ash and dread.
Each word she speaks frays on a static string.

"Tomorrow," once a promise, now a ring
of broken bells that toll inside her head.
She stands alone where the cinders still cling.

Her lips remember how to bloom in spring
a tune unlearned, a line she never read.
Each word she speaks frays on a static string.

The curtain falls. Her shadow starts to swing.
She takes her place. The lines return like thread.
She stands alone where the cinders still cling.
Each word she speaks frays on a static string.

I did not clap. I dared not break the air
her silence felt too carefully prepared.

She bowed as though the dust might lose its place,
as if the gesture held the world in grace.

The poem stuttered burnt, but she returned,
to speak the line her final breath had learned.

Perhaps she sings not words, but what they meant
the shape of fire, rehearsed in its descent.

Or maybe all she's ever called her own
is how to bow and do it all alone.

tomorrow is... my... turn to-

        She's alone no spotlight, just the sting
        of air where curtains used to rise. Instead,
        she mouths: Tomorrow is my turn to shine.

        The echoes lurch. Her voice a fractured thing,
        a loop of breath and breath that should be dead.
        She stands alone. No spotlight. Just the sting.

        Her feet repeat their bow without a king
        or queen to court her, only dust to tread.
        She mouths: Tomorrow is my turn...

        But static coats each line, a needled wing
        across her throat, unspoken words unsaid.
        She stains the silence. No spotlight. Just the sting

        a radio of ghosts still listening.
        The final word cuts out before it's read:
        She mouths tomorrow is... my... turn to
                        shine?

Will You?

He kneels at dusk with no one near.
The ring is ash. He does not mind.
He mouths the words: Will you? My dear
each syllable softened, then rewind.

The ring is ash. He does not mind.
He's certain silence is a kind of yes.
Each syllable softened, then rewind,
his jaw misremembering tenderness.

He's certain silence is a kind of yes.
The pigeons circle but do not stay.
His jaw misremembering tenderness
what fingers touched, and slipped away.

The pigeons circle but do not stay.
He sees her shadow in each stone.
What fingers touched, and slipped away
now haunt the dusk he calls his own.

He sees her shadow in each stone.
She is the yes that time denied.
Now haunt the dusk he calls his own.
He kneels. Again. The sky won't cry.

She is the yes that time denied.
He mouths the words: Will you? My dear
He kneels. Again. The sky won't cry.
He kneels at dusk with no one near.

He asked a question carved from dusk and bone,
and answered it as though he weren't alone.

No echo came. The air did not reply
but still he spoke, beneath a ringing sky.

I marked the rhythm of his kneeling form,
each "Will you?" soft as if to conjure warmth.

The ring was ash. His smile, a practiced ache.
I almost said her name. I made no break.

Will You?

He kneels at dusk with no one near.
The ring is/was a coin, or maybe a seed.
He mouths: Will you? (Will)
Time won't speak. So he does.

The ring is/was a coin, or maybe a seed.
He places it on the concrete and waits.
Time won't speak.
One word is enough. One word. Will...

He places it on the concrete and waits.
The pigeons walk through him...
They forget him instantly.

The pigeons walk through him. They forget him instantly.
Somewhere, a shadow shakes its head.
A smile grows moss behind his lips.
He's not sure what she looked like

Somewhere, a shadow shakes its head.
Yes. No. Will you. Will. You. Will.
He's not sure what she looked like, only the angle of her reply.
The loop rewinds. Or stutters. Or skips.

Yes. No. Will you. Will. You. Will.
He does not mind. He does not
He...
...kneels

Ash & Buttons

He says, It's my birthday! You're just in time.
He wears a paper crown. It sags from weather and years.
No one else is seated, but he claps. Once.

He gives you a handful of ash.
He gives you two buttons from a coat no one remembers.
He gives you a melted fork and says, Cake.
He gives you confetti made from receipts.
He gives you a balloon, invisible, but you must hold it.

He laughs like he was taught how.
He sings "Happy Birthday" to someone not here.
The tune skips, skips, loops, static
like a scratched music box choking on a candle.

He says, Make a wish!
But he doesn't blow he inhales.
The flame flickers and disappears inside his chest.

You are clapping.
You didn't start. You don't know how you learned.
Ash sticks to your palms.

He hands you a toy soldier with no head.
He says, "It's you! Everyone gets something.
Next year there will be balloons… If we're good.
If we remember how."

He gave me buttons. Gifts that could not speak.
He laughed so loud, the quiet felt too weak.

His paper crown hung sideways from his brow,
and still he said, It's mine to wear for now.

I clapped. I did. Though I had meant to wait.
He made me part of something I can't state.

I left with crumbs of joy that did not rot
but even those, I wish I had not caught.

Ash & Buttons

He says…
it's…
my…

birthday.

He claps.
No one taught him how.
The sound delays. clap (then again)
clap (echo) no echo.
You're just in time.

He gives you a

(button)

(ash…)

(you say thank you. you are wrong.)

He gives:
a melted fork (cake, it's cake he insists)
static in a box
a name no one remembers, pronounced wrong on purpose

Hold the balloon
(invisible, wheezing air)
but you do,
because it trembles when dropped.

He sings

a song with no lines

no melody

only the sound children make in dreams

before fire

before

candles

inhaled.

He says:

Make a wish.

but you wish for your hands to stop burning.

They do not.

Ash sticks where your fingers forget to be skin.

You clap.

Twice.

Just like he taught you.

It hurts. You smile.

He says: Next year there will be gifts.

If we behave.

If we deserve the buttons.

He hands you a soldier with no face.

He says: This is what you look like now.

Plates for Ghosts

Five plates, all empty.
She speaks their names to the wind.
Chairs remember weight.

A fork placed with care
though no hand will lift it now,
she smooths the silence.

Once she called for soup.
Now, her ladle holds only
reflections of breath.

She names what was loved
a doll, a sock, a wristwatch.
Each is served a seat.

Dust blesses the bread.
She cuts it like memory:
always from the crust.

Her lips move again.
This time, no names. Just humming.
The spoons tilt, listening.

She sits. She does not
eat. Her hands fold the quiet.
Then she starts again.

Five
no, four?
names unspoken.
The chairs sit each other.

A fork beside dust.
Who uses hands anymore?
She does. She does not.

Soup forgotten.
The ladle pours

She once had a doll...
Its name is now a spoon.
She feeds it silence.

Crust without center.
Knife cuts memory by weight.
No one says enough.
Spoons lean toward her hum.
It's not a song.
It's
static shaped like lullaby.

She waits.
Not for eating.
For time to close its napkin.

She set the table like a whispered hymn,
a prayer repeated where the light grew dim.

Each plate she touched became a sacred name,
though none who bore them ever truly came.

She called them once. She called them once again.
And in between, she sat with folded pain.

I nearly said I'd take the final chair.
But I just watched, and let her breathe the air.

I watched a girl recite to rows of none
her voice a loop, her spotlight long since gone.

She bowed to dust that always rose on cue,
then vanished where the stained-glass shadows grew.

The man with ring repeats his vow to air,
his bride forever absent, always there.

He kneels at dusk with tremble in his knees
the silence claps in perfect, practiced threes.

The boy with crown declares it's cake and cheer,
hands me a button: "You're my friend this year."

He spins, he laughs, then forgets his own name.
His candles flicker from imagined flame.

*A mother hums and places plates in line
each one a shape that grief has made divine.*

*She speaks five names like rosaries of breath,
and seats them all with kindness learned from death.*

*No stage, no script, yet still they take their marks,
the world rebuilt in loops, in grief, in sparks.*

*No blood remains, just memory rehearsed
not blessing, not a curse, but something worse.*

*They do not beg. They do not chase or plea.
They simply be, where being used to be.*

*And I, who watch, who write, who do not kneel,
am not more whole, just less allowed to feel.*

*Their truths perform in silence lined with thread
each gesture stitched from things they should have said.*

*I watched them spin their grief with such control
it made me wonder: who forgot the role?*

*Do they repeat because they must obey,
or did they choose to dance the same decay?*

*Is ritual the cage, or is it cure
a loop they love because it feels like sure?*

I did not write it down. I held my gaze
to walls where soot still sang of brighter days.

Their silence burned. Their hush became a blade.
But even now, I'm glad I stayed.

The voices turned to shadow, not to light.
And still I walk, though not from fear or flight.

I walk because the air has changed its skin.
It sings now not with voice, but deep within.

I hear a laugh that isn't mine, but known.
A whisper curling from a broken phone.

The next place isn't loud, but something waits
a doorless hall with many listening gates.

They told me breath is just a song delayed.
I go now where the echo doesn't fade.

So take these bones, these verses I still keep
and follow me into the rooms that weep.

The Room of Laughter

The door opened sideways,
like a shrug.
No handle just the hush of dust parting.

Inside, the air was warm,
not with heat,
but with something that used to follow sunlight.

And then
the laughter.

It came not from a mouth,
but from the walls themselves,
soft and spinning,
the sound of a child who had not yet learned
what laughter costs.

A high pitch,
cracked at the edges,
then doubled over with breathless joy
like running without shoes,
like falling on grass and not crying.

It looped.
Not perfectly.
Each time the giggle caught in its throat
a half-second sooner.

And still, they stood there
those without lungs,
without mouths,
just listening.

One reached out not to touch,
but to feel the echo
brush their fingers like warm ribbon.

No one moved.
Not even me.
It was not grief.
It was permission.

We did not speak.
We could not.
Laughter like that
cannot be followed.

It must be carried.

<u>Antiphon I - The Echo of Joy</u>

Who was she, the one who laughed?

She was the sun inside a breath.
She was the game before the rules.
She was the warmth we could not keep.

Why do we listen?

Because it does not ask.
Because it does not accuse.
Because it does not stop.

I felt it bloom and vanish in my chest
a laugh not mine, but close enough to rest.

No joy survives the fall in perfect form,
and yet it played like breath that stayed warm.

The dead stood still, as if to let it pass,
like wind through reeds, or light through broken glass.

I did not weep. I did not write it down.
Some sounds are best left holy, soft, and crown.

But even joy leaves footprints in its wake.
The next room waits. And it will ask what broke.

The Room of Apology

She spoke from the ceiling,
or maybe the floor.
The sound had no center.
Only ache.

I'm sorry.
I didn't mean to.
I didn't.
I didn't.

Her voice was threadbare,
the kind that once wrapped around a child's hand
but now just looped around air.

I'm sorry.
I shouldn't have gone.
I thought I locked the door.

No image came with it.
No screen.
No photo.
Only sound.

And still the dead gathered
not to judge,
but to remember
how it felt
to need forgiveness.

One knelt.
One placed a stone
against the wall
and whispered nothing.

I'm sorry.
I didn't know.
I left the stove on.
I left the light.
I left.

Some apologies are so old
they echo without end.

Some are still being answered.
Just not here.
Not yet.

<u>*Antiphon II - Chorus of the Unanswered*</u>

We heard her say "I'm sorry"
and we remembered what it meant.

We heard her say "I left the light"
and we remembered darkness first.

We heard her say "I didn't know"
and we remembered that we did.

She said it again.
We stayed anyway.

Forgiveness floats, but sorrow tends to sink.
The next room waits with heavier things to think.

The Room of Regret

I should have turned around.
I should have said
I should have

The voice stumbles,
not with fear,
but with memory too heavy to name.

I knew something was wrong
but I smiled.
That was easier.
That was

It pauses at the same place
every time.
A single breath
that never lands.

I told myself I'd go back.
I didn't.
She asked me to stay.
I didn't.
She

The dead don't cry here.
They just listen
with the kind of stillness
that forgives nothing
but understands everything.

A cracked photograph rests beneath a speaker.
No one touches it.
Even the breathless know shame
when they see it frame itself.

I could've.
I would've.
I-

The tape continues.
The voice keeps trying.
The silence keeps forgiving.
But the door behind me
doesn't close.

Antiphon III - The Last Story

We turned too late.
We spoke too slow.
We said "I will"
and then let go.

We tried to warn.
We tried to stay.
But time, like us,
decayed away.

It tells the story.
It breaks the breath.
It asks no questions.
It tastes like death.

Some voices fade, but never find release.
They echo not for comfort, but for peace.

The laugh, the plea, the pause that cracked with weight
they stitched my ribs with threads I can't translate.

Regret, it seems, does not require a name.
It folds itself in breath, then speaks in flame.

And I, who only came to write it down,
have swallowed more than ink could ever drown.

These rooms don't offer answers just the cost
of what we failed to say before we lost.

But I have heard the dead in how they wait.
And now I go to meet the one who threads fate.

The Seamstress of Bone

She sat beneath a ribcage strung with thread,
her needle humming songs that had no name,
her thimble carved from something once called dead.

Around her feet, the breathless came the same
not begging, not in pain, but simply still,
as if to stitch was holier than flame.

Her gown was scraps of sorrow, cloth, and will.
One sleeve was laced with names, the other bare.
Her spool unwound like time that won't be still.

She said, "You've brought your voice, so bring your care.
My needle doesn't ask what should be kept.
It only asks what silence you can wear."

I spoke of rooms where memory still wept,
of laughter looped, of echoes barely whole.
She smiled, and with her thread, the distance leapt.

"Then tell me what you'd trade to make you whole
a word unsaid, a grief too old to teach?
Or shall I sew the mouth and free the soul?"

I flinched. She laughed. Her hands began to reach
for threads that shimmered sinew, smoke, regret
and pulled from me a breath too thin for speech.

"You write," she said, "but ink is not truth yet.
The page forgets, the page can lie, betray.
I sew in skin. My gospel stays when wet."

"Each wound I stitch is one you give away.
Each thread, a vow to vanish what you fear.
Do you consent to silence, poet? Say."

I asked her what the dead did when drawn near.
She paused her voice a whisper in the thread:
"They ask for names. And sometimes, they appear."

"Some come for peace, but others come instead
to feel again the weight of what they lost
not resurrection, but a softer dread."

"I sew a mother's lullaby in frost,
a soldier's laugh along a broken seam.
I mend the shape of love, but not its cost."

"You poets gather ash and call it dream.
I gather ash and bind it to the breath.
Your ink dissolves. My thread redeems the theme."

Her voice was calm. Her gaze, as still as death.
She gestured to the walkers standing close
each draped in fabric stitched from former deaths.

One bore a sleeve of children's names in rows.
One wore a patch of paper, torn and bled.
Another's collar held her sister's ghost.

"They came to me with words they could not shed,"
she said. "And now they wear them without weight.
The living choke. The dead remember thread."

"I do not judge. I do not mediate.
I offer only rest from what won't sleep
the names that burn, the thoughts that come too late."

I asked her if she dreamed, or if she'd keep
a piece of me if I gave in to thread.
She said, "I only dream when I don't weep."

"But yes, I'll take the part you cannot shed
the part that writes instead of letting go.
I'll stitch it in the quiet of the dead."

She showed me then a square as white as snow.
"This is for those who almost chose to stay,
but feared what they might be if they said no."

Her fingers moved with ease, like dusk through day.
She stitched a line that shimmered in the air:
"Here lies the poet who would not look away."

I asked, *"Have you been stitched?" She said, "I wear
the very first regret this world forgot.
It keeps me warm. It keeps my needle fair."

"You speak of grief as if it can be caught.
It can't. But it can dress the ones who stay.
And I have dressed them all, in what was not."

I touched her work. The thread began to fray
not poorly sewn, but soft with something real:
the trembling wish of words we couldn't say.

I felt a knot inside begin to heal,
not disappear, but shift beneath the skin.
The wound remained, but now it knew to kneel.

I turned to go. She did not ask again.
She smiled and placed her needle in her palm.
The choir outside resumed its breathless hymn.

She whispered, "Wear your ink. It is your psalm.
But know I keep your silence in my thread.
Return to me when stillness feels like balm."

And so I left still breathing, but half-fed,
a single stitch undone along my side,
and every step still whispering her thread.

The thread is tied. The ink has dried. I see what breaks does not end. It returns to be.

Last Breath, First Word

Something grew
in the places
we forgot to curse.

We didn't recognize it at first
too soft, too bright,
too pretty to be trusted
too full of life

But it didn't ask.

It just grew.

*I've watched them burn, and bleed and bend
now every tale returns to me again.*

*I told their stories, carved each name with care.
But ink runs dry when no one else is there.*

*I wandered long enough to survive the fight
I suppose I am all there is left to write.*

*So this one's mine. My breath and my scars.
I'll leave a light, wherever lights still are.*

*The ghosts have sung. The pages have turned.
The towns erased. The cities not returned.*

*I've followed maps that led to dust and stone,
and learned that memory survives alone.*

*I've spoken softly, stayed behind the frame,
while others walked through fire to earn a name.*

*But still I breathed. And held the thread.
A witness is a kind of voice for the dead.*

*I've written of the kindness that betrayed,
the silence that remembered how we prayed.*

I kept my distance just enough to see,
and now the only subject left is me.

So here I am. No mask, gate or guise,
just what remains beneath a poet's eyes.

Not hero. Not survivor. Not a spark.
Just someone writing poems alone in the dark.

I do not know what happens after this.
A future lives beyond a page like mist.

But if you find these words, and you still breathe
then let this be the thread I choose to leave.

Don't write me back. Don't draw a grave or shrine.
Just live. Just walk. And let your voice be mine.

The Last Poet

The last poet walked where steel once spoke
now quiet, under vines that burst like hymns.
A streetlamp wore a crown of fern and smoke,
its bulb a nest for wrens whose throats brimmed
with echoes, not of war, but rain.
The poet knelt. The earth forgave again.

Beneath their feet, the roots had cracked the bone
of boardroom, courthouse, market stall.
They passed a bank whose roof was overgrown
coins rusted soft, the moss had claimed them all.
O Earth, the poet sang, this feast is yours
these towers fall to feed your sacred spores.

No scaffold now, no tower, trench, or trade
just vines that wrapped around old stone and will.
A freeway, coiled in ivy's green cascade,
whispered tales in leaves, alive and still.
Forgive us, breathed the last of human rhyme,
we paved you over, calling theft 'divine.'

They found a statue, half-subsumed in leaf
a general pointing, blind to his defeat.
His face eroded into moss and grief,
his medals melted where the lichen meet.
O Time, they said, you give what man denied
you turn their pride to petals when they've died.

And oh, the gardens blooming through the bones
orchids in doorways, birch in courthouse halls.
The world reborn in quiet, tangled tones,
not carved by kings but sung through waterfall.
A throne of stone? The roots will split it clean.
No crown endures the wild and growing green.

They mourned not just the cities swallowed whole
but hearts that beat in conquest, not in grace.
A race that tried to own what made it whole,
yet failed to see the mirror in its place.
We took, and called it growth, and left you dry.
Forgive us. Let this garden be reply.

The poet leaves verses in the moss,
no need for fame, no need to mourn the loss.

The trees grew thick where towers once had soared,
a cradle green where silence was restored.

The soil forgave. The sky forgot our claim.
No flag remained. No record kept our name.

But echoes roam where steel once kissed the air,
and whisper truths we dared not speak nor bear.

A final bloom where monuments once lay
the dead don't rise, but memories decay.

So let the roots rewrite what we once knew.
The last word fell, but something still came through.

breathe in

what's

left

Canto VIII - Remnants

Beneath the skyline's hum, the sirens slept
The pigeons bloomed like ash across the street
And lovers' vows in glass reflections wept.

The clocks all chimed a rhythm too complete,
Repeating fate as headlines turned to ink,
Where news and time and dreams began to meet.

She carved an ode in steam upon the sink
"To city's breath, and love, and neon glow"
While certainty collapsed into a blink

The playground twisted in a rust-red throe.
One child stared blankly, teeth behind a hum,
And bit the hand that used to help him grow.

The towers trembled as the sirens drum
A broadcast voice fell fractured in the static
The screens all burned with headlines yet to come.

A thousand feet in flight, both wild and frantic
The subway roared with passengers turned grey
Each face was lost, each scream abrupt and manic.

A doctor whispered, "There's no more delay."
His gloves still on, he knelt beside the glass,
A dying world caught mid-report today.

The cop said, "Tell my son he'll have to pass "
Then bled across the stairs without a name.
Still gripping one blank ticket for the mass.

A politician cried but played the game
He raised the flag, then fled into the sea,
His final lie a flicker lost to flame.

"We are the swarm, and we remember thee,"
The voices chanted from a broken throat,
"A million minds in one, and none are free."

A house collapsed beneath a dusty moat,
Where echoes wandered in a silent line,
And shoes still marched though none had cast a vote.

He found a photograph of "Doing Fine,"
A store ad wrapped around a starving man
The ink said "Hope," the image drew a sign.

A cracked cathedral marked the caravan
Of hollow souls that walked with boots of ash,
Led by a girl who muttered, "Yes, I can."

A priest with broken glasses made a stash
Of scripture burnt, and whispered it in code,
While drawing angels in the mud and trash.

A wall declared: "The Zone Will Share the Load,"
But inside walls, the food was weighed with guilt
And justice wore a suit too finely sewed.

They drank to peace in glasses softly gilt,
Then locked the gates to those who coughed too loud,
The courtroom blessed the scaffold they had built.

One poet spoke, though heads began to crowd:
"No paradise survives on silence bled,
No truth exists beneath a plastic shroud."

He trusted one who kissed, then left instead
A traitor's flame that licked the final rope,
And danced among the ruins where he bled.

The air itself had nothing left but smoke
A loop of cries beneath a shattered dome
Each echo fading faster as it spoke.

He found a wall and carved the word: go home
Though none remained to read it or believe,
The line became a prayer beneath the loam.

A violet bloomed beneath a poet's sleeve,
Each petal a vow the end could not deceive.

The stone still wept with dreams it could not keep,
while trees beneath began to stretch from sleep.

They'd waited long beneath the soot and steel,
while man forgot the roots beneath his heel.

And when the towers groaned and dropped their name,
the forest stepped through cracks no wall could tame.

No war declared, no fanfare marked their claim
just leaf, and claw, and moss that learned our frame.

So silence bloomed where sirens used to scream.
The woods returned, not vengeance, but a dream.

Forests and Feral Things

The trees returned with roots that cracked the stone.
They split through walls and curled through traffic lights.
Their leaves turned buildings into overgrown.

I watched one vine consume a bus in nights.
Its petals bloomed from rust like painted skin.
Its tendrils whispered over shattered flights.

No longer tamed, the woods began to win.
They swallowed roads, rewrote the borders drawn.
The fields now hummed where cities once had been.

The foxes came and hunted well before dawn.
Their eyes were not afraid of human scent.
They marked the malls with footprints, lithe and strong.

I passed a pond where deer moved confident
across a gas station submerged in moss.
Their breath was calm. Their bodies held no bent.

A snake lay coiled atop a steel exhaust.
Its tongue flicked toward the ruined checkout gate.
The register was blank. The wires lost.

I saw a bear patrol a chapel's slate.
It slept inside a pulpit carved in oak.
Its growls replaced the echo of debate.

One owl took up its roost in broken smoke.
It nested in the crown of a machine.
Its wings beat soft above the shattered yoke.

And there, amidst the green that split the screen,
a girl was painting animals in ash.
She said, "They've come to cleanse what might have been."

She wore a mask made from a paper sash.
She kept a mouse inside her coat for luck.
Her prayers were leaves she whispered in a flash.

A group of boys had trained with knives and muck
not to defend, but learn the way of roots.
They studied trails, the language of the buck.

They named the stars not after men in suits,
but after types of wind, of moss, of night.
They slept in trees and carried dried-out fruits.

One shrine they built was made of bone and light
a circle ringed with feathers and old tools.
They left it open only once a rite.

I found a boy who'd catalogued the ghouls
of forest lore his journal bound in bark.
He drew the shapes of monsters, dreams, and rules.

One drawing bore the title: Past the Ark.
It showed a woman made of smoke and vine.
He said, "She walks where skies forget to mark."

The animals had no need to define
what we had lost or wasted, burned or swore.
They simply lived, and thus became divine.

A lynx was spotted where the dam once roared.
It drank where oil had spilled for decades straight.
It blinked, then vanished through the green-stained floor.

A child ran barefoot through a woodland gate.
She said the woods would guard her in return.
She fed a fox, then left with silent gait.

I carved a stanza in the curve of fern.
I watched it curl as if it read the line.
I did not ask, but wondered what it learned.

I walked along the forest spine,
no longer sure if I was guest or prey
just one more voice beneath a vine-strung sign.

The world we built had been the world in sway.
Now nature spoke, not cruel but never tame.
Its breath returned, and took no bribes to stay.

I sat where moss had made a throne from stone,
No crown, no court, just silence all my own.

The vines had climbed the scaffolds we had raised,
And bloomed through wires once meant to frame our praise.

The air was thick with scent of bark and dew,
A breath the world had saved when we withdrew.

No engines spoke, no signal cracked the dawn,
Just birds rehearsing notes we'd called long gone.

I used to write for eyes behind a screen
For crowds, for pages stamped, for what had been.

But now my pen was stitched from cedar smoke,
And every line I wrote began to soak.

I wrote on leaves, on trunks, on fossilled light,
And each reply came slow, but came out right.

The earth did not applaud, or even nod
But when I paused, the sky replaced "O God."

I wept, not from regret but from release.
The war of wanting had made room for peace.

The deer approached and listened with one ear.
She did not flee. She did not come too near.

She simply stood, a page without a crease.
I wrote no ode. Just felt the moment cease.

And then a wind began to trace my skin,
Not cold, not warm, just asking to begin.

"You've walked," it said, "and named what grief has burned.
But now the world speaks back. It is your turn."

I knelt and dipped my hand in dirt and seed.
I let the sentence fail. I let it bleed.

I wrote not who, not when, but only here.
I carved the now, not future, into clear.

A root curled round my boot, then touched my heel.
The forest claimed me. Not to take, but heal.

The wolves did not arrive with snarls or might.
They came to watch me vanish into light.

The girl returned, her fox beside her path.
She nodded once, then smeared my verse in ash.

"You've written much," she said. "Now leave it be.
The world you knew has bent into the tree."

I who walked through flame, stone, and storm
Unclenched my grip on language, line, and form.

Something Green Has Learned to Breathe Again

Something green has learned to breathe again.
It cracks the stone, then waits beneath our feet.
I dare not ask if it is foe or friend.

The streets are vines. The cities have no men.
The trees return to places built for heat.
Something green has learned to breathe again.

A moss-wrapped bone still whispers like a pen.
A sprout curls through the corner of defeat.
I dare not ask if it is foe or friend.

A bird now nests where guards once counted ten.
A field has grown where silence used to eat.
Something green has learned to breathe again.

We walk, unsure, through thorns that don't condemn.
The air is wrong, but not yet incomplete.
I dare not ask if it is foe or friend.

We plant, though what will bloom may not be men.
The soil forgets. The seed does not repeat.
Something green has learned to breathe again.
I dare not ask if it is foe or friend.

and so, it breathes.

I did not choose to survive.

I simply stayed one breath longer than the silence.

That was enough.

If you have read these colors, if the words held even briefly in your hands before drifting back to ash, then something of us is still moving. That is all we ever asked.

Not rescue. Not restoration. Only witness.

The world we knew was louder than it deserved to be. We wrapped ourselves in noise and light and called it peace.

But the truth was always quieter. It was gray. It was the shape of a small child's hand on a broken window.

It was how people betray each other with rules.

How hope returns disguised as something strange and green and unasked for.

I offer no answers, only fragments.

If your breath caught while reading, then you and I have shared the oldest ritual: we remembered something that tried to disappear.

And so this ends. Not with salvation or with warning, but with a door to new life. You may open it. Or not.

The choice is yours.

Take it gently. Take it forward. Let it bleed new light.

Epilogue: The World Reads On

The book lay buried, folded into ash.
No reader sought it. No hand turned a page.
It pulsed beneath the roots in silent flash.

A storm passed over, peeling back the sage
of moss that crowned the hill where stanzas slept.
The dirt forgot its name, forgot its age.

And yet, the poem held. The ink had wept
into the fibers of a shirt once worn.
Its rhymes were bent, its chorus roughly kept.

A fox passed by, its fur like dusk and thorn.
It paused. It sniffed the cloth and stirred no fear.
It trod again, but not as one forlorn.

A rain came next. It pooled, then disappeared.
The drops fell soft, then stung, then sang like glass.
They did not read, but something in them steered.

One root grew down where metaphors once pass
it touched a line and branched, as if to spread
a syntax made of water, breath, and grass.

No bell was rung. No voice called out the dead.
No scholar wept. No altar bore the text.
But still the poem stirred inside its bed.

A beetle crawled across a phrase and flexed
its wings against the word endure half-lost.
Its carapace turned stanzas into hexed.

Above, the stars wheeled through their silent frost.
No longer watched, they did not dim or speak.
Yet constellations formed without exhaust.

A single cloud rolled westward for a week.
Its shape recalled the curve of cursive ink.
Its edges mimicked verses not yet weak.

The world had healed, not clean, not quick, not pink
with springtime dreams but quiet in its crawl.
No cities stood. No leaders left to link.

Yet here and there, in cracks of wall on wall,
a line appeared that no one carved or planned.
Be kind, it said. Or Leave the fire tall.

The wind arranged old feathers in the sand.
They shaped a stanza none alive had taught.
A dog walked past, then turned, as if it scanned.

And in a cave, in stone with lichen caught,
an antler etched with stammered poetry
was found by someone born of ash and thought.

She did not know the tongue, nor "lyric" be
but understood the pause, the breath, the break.
She traced the shape, then copied it in tree.

Another found a mask near frozen lake
and scratched her name in soot beside a rhyme.
She did not ask what gods the words might wake.

In months to come, they gathered fragments' chime
in teeth, in glass, in bark, in wires bent.
They stitched new ballads out of what lost time.

No one declared, "Here's what the poem meant."
They sang instead: It lived, and so do we.
They added lines, unsure of their intent.

A child repeated, "Stars can learn to see."
He hummed in triplets, danced in loops and clicks.
He buried shells in patterns by a tree.

The elders watched, still limping on their sticks.
They taught no grammar, only how to stop
and listen when the syllables would fix.

A new one carved his birth into a crop.
Another painted verse in fishbone white.
They marked their silence like a sacred shop.

And when the wind grew loud on certain nights,
they gathered near where no one marked a grave.
They did not speak. They shared each other's lights.

No name was read. No verse was meant to save.
But still, the rhythm held within their hands.
They moved like language long beyond the wave.

The book was gone. The poet joined the sands.
But every breath that carried rhyme or hush
reformed the lines in ways no mind commands.

So though the world grew silent, slow, and crushed
a pulse remains in every leaf and dune.
It is not loud, but it is wide and lush.

It sings beneath the bones of rain and rune.
It speaks in shapes no lexicon could bind.
It waits, not as a truth, but as a tune.

The world forgets. The stars go deaf and blind.
But once there was a voice that walked before.
It did not fade. It left its breath behind that still believes.

That breath was caught in reeds beside a shore,
where no one came, but still the waves would bow.
A wind composed its verse and offered more.

A turtle passed, its shell engraved with now.
No hand had carved it, but the script was true
a mark of life that did not ask for vow.

A glacier split and sang its thundering cue.
Its echo rolled through valleys deep with moss.
Inside the crack, a rhyming shimmer grew.

A girl drew patterns near a mountain cross.
She'd never read, but knew the cadence well.
Her fingers shaped the words without a loss.

Each child born would learn how voices dwell
in firelight flickers, or in beetle wings.
They'd mark with mud where earlier breath once fell.

A boy once danced around a pile of springs
and shouted words that matched no known refrain.
Still, others joined. It hummed in copper rings.

And so the poem, loosed from tongue and brain,
was not recited but became a feel
a way to walk, to mourn, to breathe, remain.

One elder drew three circles with her heel
and said, "This is the name of those we miss."
She wept, and others wept, and none would kneel.

The stars grew dimmer, yet not lost in bliss.
They pulsed not meaning, but a quiet dare
a rhythm matching grief with something kissed.

The rivers, too, began to write in air.
Their swells grew slow, but sang along the reeds.
Each turn a line, each ripple a small prayer.

And I was there though scattered into seeds
remain in how they rest, in how they try,
in how they name what every silence needs.

No one recalls the who, or even why.
They only know that when the dusk is near,
a shape of sound returns beneath the sky.

A kind of verse too open to be clear.
A kind of truth too soft to bend or kill.
A kind of echo shaped to mean: We're here.

The world reads on. It doesn't read with will.
It doesn't need the ink, or even page.
It doesn't learn the rhymes but holds them still.

It sings not loud, but through the quiet sage.
The poem lives, unwritten, after age.

A silence, then another voice

We Are What Remains When Memory Breaks

We are the breath that never left the throat.
We are the name no prayer dared to quote.
We are the hands that knock but do not plead.
We are the mouths unmade by hunger's need.

We are the teeth that chewed on godless dawn.
We are the dream you kept the lights upon.
We are the rhythm tucked inside your floor.
We are the math that makes your losses four.

We do not crave. We do not mourn. We do
not seek revenge. We seek what once was true.
We do not bleed. We do not rot for show.
We are the proof of what you chose to know.

Your walls were rules.
Your gates were stitched with shame.
Your silences were branded into flame.
You told your children nothing but the wait.
You locked the doors and said it wasn't fate.

We heard you.
In the pauses. In the light.
In the songs you didn't sing each night.
We gathered in the corners of your eyes.
We learned to mimic lullabies.

We do not ask. We have no need to speak.
We are the tone inside your father's cheek
when he said "not now," and meant "never."
We are the quiet. But we remember.

You built your shelters out of shattered prayer.
We grew our teeth from absence and the air.
You fed the fire every friend you knew.
We kept the ash and made it something new.

We are the voice that never breaks or begs.
We are the mirror filled with different legs.
We are the code inside your child's hum.
We are what answers when the silence comes.

We do not leave. We do not need to stay.
We are the price for looking far away.
We are not gone. We only sleep in wait.
We are not dead.
We are what death creates.

If I am gone, let this remain
a shape of hope, a thread of flame.

Each breath is a poem I've given back.
Let it echo, even if it cracks.

Not all who break forget to sing.
Some colors shine in suffering.

If you can still hear them,
Sing back.

Sincerely,
The Last Poet

Acknowledgements

This book was written in silence, mostly at night.
Only a few people knew I was doing it at all.

Thank you to my grandmother, who has always known exactly what I am writing, and when I am writing it. Her encouragement comes with the persistence of gentle nagging, and somehow, that's what keeps me going. She asks for updates before I realize I have any.
She reminds me, without ever saying it, that someone is waiting for the words.

This book was stitched together from ruin, breath, and memory.
And though I wrote it quietly, it was never written alone.

Thank you, always.

Don't forget to breathe.

About the Author

E. C. Mira is a poet and creative whose work explores the space between silence and survival, memory and ruin. In *Remnants*, she weaves her love of literature, art, and form into a lyrical narrative of what endures after the world ends. Her writing is rooted in reflection, emotion, and the strange beauty of ordinary things especially when viewed through the lens of collapse.

When she's not writing, Mira enjoys reading, gardening, crocheting, and watching horror films. A devoted planner and diary-keeper, she draws inspiration from the rhythm of routine and the quiet magic of unpredictability.

Other Work

The Seasons in Poetry
- Spring: The Anthology
- Summer: The Anthology
- Autumn: The Anthology
- Winter: The Anthology (Jan. 2026)

Summer Shadows
- Final Recollections
- Room Without Walls
- Thorns on the Widow's Veil
- Through the Glass
- Dreamscapes and Daylight
- She Chooses Back
- The Siren's Lure
- Echoes of the Forgotten Gods
- Oblivion is a Mercy
- The Spiral Diary
- The Moon is a Keyhole
- Voices in the Static
- When the Bell Rings at Midnight

www.ingramcontent.com/pod-product-compliance
Lightning Source LLC
Chambersburg PA
CBHW030817090426
42737CB00009B/764